"This book is painfully tru
speaks to the open wounds and the process of healing as a woman
in a Mexican family. This book beautifully exemplifies a reflection
of the self, the human experience, self-hate, self-love, gender
biases and forgiveness."

– Dr. María Elena Cruz
San José State University

«... el compartir poemas de lucha, de la importancia del papel de
la mujer y de muchos temas más nos transmite fuerza para seguir
abriendo caminos y oportunidades como ella lo ha hecho para las
mujeres latinas.»

– Erica Fernández
Stanford University

«El trabajo de Elvira toca el alma de sus lectores y oyentes, en
español and in English. La habilidad de trascender idiomas y
llegar a las emociones de una audiencia multilingüe no es fácil de
lograr. Sin embargo, Elvira es capaz de hablar directamente con
nuestros corazones e inspirarnos a continuar nuestra lucha diaria
a través de sus poemas y ensayos.»

– Dr. Diego Román
Southern Methodist University

"Elvira's words have drifted into my mind and embedded
themselves in my soul. Every sentence is gently crafted with love
and a fiery spirit that can affect even the hardest of hearts. Her
stories tell the sometimes difficult, the sometimes beautiful, and
overall necessary perspective that needs to be told."

– Norma González
Stanford University

AN (IM)POSSIBLE LIFE

Poesía y Testimonio in the Borderlands

Cover, dibujitos, and book design by César Torres, www.cearto.com
Project management and production by David Patiño

Elvira Prieto
Visit my website at www.elviraprieto.com

Printed in the United States of America

ISBN-13 978-1517074463
ISBN-10 1517074460

First edition, first printing, October 2015

Cover photo: The cover image is of Elvira's maternal grandmother, Dolores Gallegos de Reyes in 1947. Dolores is sitting with her four eldest children (L to R) Evangelina, Mario, Erasmo, and Arturo. Dolores is pregnant with Elvira's mother, Guadalupe. The picture was taken to send to Elvira's grandfather, Felipe Reyes, who was working as a laborer in the United States as part of the Bracero Program.

*For You
and For Me,
with all my Love, Blessings, and Light.*

CONTENTS
***

4 New York

5 *Reflejos*

6 *Besitos*

7 *Amig@s*

***

Preface: *Mi Vida*

The story of my life is about hardship, humility, education, and love. I am the daughter of peasants. I was born and raised in California's Central San Joaquin Valley, in a family of immigrant farm workers from Mexico. I could call that the beginning but it is not. The beginning of my experience started before I was born. It is affected by the lives of my parents and their families and the reasons that pulled them to the United States. I come from a long line of fighters. Women who have suffered, struggled, and overcome with love. Love for their children, love for other people's children, love for themselves, and love for their community.

I begin with my maternal great grandmother inspired by her life story, passed down to me through my mother and other women in our family. Her name was Lolita, short for Dolores. Lolita married young, birthed thirteen children, and tragically became a widow when her eldest son was still only in his teens. My great grandmother buried her husband and raised her children on her own.

Lolita gave birth to my grandmother—also named Dolores. The second Lolita married and started her own family at the age of thirteen. From my mother's stories I learned about my grandmother's tireless work to send her children to school in Mexico. Whenever there was a new mayor in the city nearest their small rural town, my grandmother, a laborer with a third grade education, travelled into the city to meet the new government official and advocate for her children. She always returned with boxes of donated pencils and notebooks for her children, and the children of other families in her community, because they could not afford to buy basic school supplies. My grandmother's tireless efforts and dedication came to fruition through her family. All of her children were able to receive a middle school education and technical training. Her eldest daughter and son became elementary school teachers and eventually school directors in their rural community.

I am inspired by my grandmother's determination to fight for the equity of resources her children deserved. The stories told by family members who knew her help me understand how she served to inspire others as well. She was viewed as a leader in the community and many people loved her because she willingly and actively gave of herself. She shared everything she had with the neighboring families who were worse off than her own. «*Ella trabajaba en el campo como un hombre*» "She worked in the fields like a man", my mother tells me. My grandmother died from a massive heart attack at the young age of fifty-three, having raised nine children, a multitude of grandchildren, and having cared for an ill and bedridden husband for thirty years. I was present at her funeral in Chihuahua. I was a child, yet I vividly remember the endless mass of people who walked to and cried at her gravesite. In visits to my mother's hometown as an adult I have asked family members about this memory. «*Todos fueron al entierro de Doña Lolita*» "Everyone went to Doña Lolita's funeral." My mother explained that everyone referred to at least a thousand people from the surrounding communities.

It is important for me to talk about my grandmother as I describe myself, because she gave her experiences and values to my mother who then passed them on to me. When I think about my own sense of responsibility to the larger communities in which I live, I know it is something I both inherited *de mis antepasados*, from past generations, and gained from the direct example set by my parents.

The experiences of my parents in Mexico and the U.S. are a part of my life as much as their own. Growing up my father constantly reminded my siblings and me that even though we were born in the U.S., «*no se les olvide que son mexicanos*» "do not forget that you are Mexican." He made certain we learned how to eat the spiciest chile he could find—one of the subtle ways in which we were to prove our identity, our Mexican-ness. We also listened, sang, and danced to all types of *música mexicana*, learned about the food, the customs, and the history of our *familia* and *México*. Most importantly our parents wanted us to maintain the language they taught us, as this would prove to be our primary means of communication with our immediate and extended family and cultural ties to Mexico. My mother and father insisted we speak only Spanish at home. In their eyes, forgetting the language equated being ashamed of our background as well as permanently severing our connection to family.

For a long time I saw my father's way as simply too strict and sexist, especially since it meant that as Mexican children we were subjected to an extreme patriarchal system of rules of conduct and behavior. We were his property — my siblings, my mother, and me — and we were not allowed to question his demands or point of view. My father saw any type of behavior that did not follow his rules as Anglo-like and disrespectful. I disagreed with him constantly and found myself caught between wanting to maintain my identity as a *mexicana* but also wanting the sense of freedom that was supposed to accompany my citizenship in the United States. Despite our ideological differences, I believe my father was successful in teaching my siblings and me to be proud of our background. I am grateful for the part of my upbringing that gave me a cultural and language base from which my Chicana identity emerged. I was made to see early on that by virtue of being born and raised in the U.S., in Mexico I would never be fully seen as a *mexicana*. Likewise, in the U.S., I would never be fully accepted as American because I am not white.

My family spent a period of nine months living in Guadalajara, Jalisco, between my third and fourth birthdays. My parents took us to Mexico from our birthplace in Reedley, California, in order to give life in their home country another try. They never intended to stay in the U.S. permanently. Like many *mexicano* immigrants their initial migration to this country was intended as a temporary means to help their family financially. Unfortunately, the return to Mexico did not prove economically successful; thus, they were pulled back to California.

My father returned to the States first, in order to secure work and find a place for us to live. My siblings and I were left with my mother, under the responsibility of my father's family. My earliest memories begin there. I remember assuming I was born in Mexico until the time my father came back to return us to California. Our neighborhood friends let us know they felt deserted by our impending departure by teasing us. They told us we did not belong in Mexico with them because we were not *mexicanos*, and surely we must think we were better just because we were from *el norte*, the north. I was shocked. Of course I was *mexicana*, that is what my parents were, and I didn't even know how to speak English. I could not possibly be an *americana* and belong in *el norte*.

I heard many wonderful stories about *el norte*, however, so my excitement at the prospect of going there soon took away the hurt feelings left by my peers. The stories we heard were like many shared between other immigrant families coming to the United States from all corners of the world. It was the land of opportunity, and if we worked hard enough, we would have all the things we lacked in Mexico: sufficient food, shelter, safety, and comfort.

Our trip back to California was full of trauma, angst, and fear. My siblings and I were separated from my parents when we arrived at the border. My parents were not yet legal residents and had to get across the border by different means. Since my siblings and I had our birth certificates we were simply driven across by my parent's friends and taken to a paternal uncle's home in Los Angeles. We waited in agony for my parent's arrival. I was overcome with anxiety and horror upon being separated from my mother and left with strangers. I did not understand what my parents were doing. I suppose it is better that I not know the danger they were exposed to, in the desire to give us a better life in the U.S.

I learned the value of humility as a result of growing up poor and working from a very young age. I started working in grape fields with my parents at about the same time I started attending school. The physical pain and exhaustion I felt taught me many valuable lessons. One of the factors that made me want to succeed in school was the belief that it was the only way out of such meager working conditions. My parents constantly reminded us that if we wanted to make something better of our lives, we had to go to school and we had to excell. Their reminders usually came when we questioned the fact that we had to work so hard, and yet could not afford to do the fun things our schoolmates and friends always talked about: going to the movies, going on vacations, going out to eat at restaurants. We talked about all of these things as we worked and made plans for our futures as a means to break the monotony of our labor. The need to succeed in education is very real when you experience such a bleak alternative.

Even though my family rarely made more than $10,000 a year, my parents believed so firmly in the opportunity an education could provide us that they only asked us to work after school, on weekends, and during school breaks. My father looked for work on farms within the nearest communities and in between seasons he did not work because there were no crops available. My mother was able to convince him that uprooting the family in order to migrate after crops, like so many other immigrant families had to do, would have a disastrous impact on our education.

My mother played a key role in instilling her belief in education on my father, and exhorted the limited control she had over our futures by convincing him of this. As a result she had to do that much more with limited resources, and she had to make sure we had enough to eat and clothes to wear, so that my father would not feel he wasn't providing enough for his family. This allowed him to face the men of the families who did uproot their children because they could not survive on what we earned. Other community members constantly told my father how amazed they were by his ability to provide for us. All the credit was given to my father, when in reality my mother's frugality and creativity was central to our survival.

I have known the responsibility of caring for others, more vulnerable than myself since I can remember. When I was five, I helped potty train my sister. She is a year and five months younger than me. I cleaned out her potty and wiped her behind. When I was six, my baby brother was born. My mother was very ill, so I was responsible for helping to care for both my mother and the newborn. I counted out her cocktail of medications and learned to hand-wash soiled cloth diapers. Throughout my childhood, I remember having to clean up other people's vomit. My father and uncle's hangover vomit. My mother's asthma attack induced vomit. My brother's and sister's stomach flu vomit. I held my breath and managed somehow to keep myself from vomiting.

I am an educator. I have worked with pre-school to college-age students in schools and communities across this country. This is a labor of love. I get my heart broken regularly. I am filled with love and inspiration every day. There is nothing easy about this. I can relate to so much of what my students live through. I choose to do this work because I believe in the power of equitable education to provide increased socio-economic and life opportunities for children from backgrounds like my own. I also understand that our educational system is currently not the great equalizer. I was the first woman in my family to go to college. I have a B.A. from Stanford and an Ed.M. from Harvard. These degrees are noteworthy because I earned them even when others thought I did not deserve them. I have benefited directly from the opportunities access to higher education can provide, and yet I have borne witness to the manner in which many young people from backgrounds like my own are disillusioned and disenfranchised every day. I have seen firsthand the manner in which children's spirits are broken by inadequate educational resources and teaching, as well as constant social deprivation, poverty, and neglect. At the same time I am equally inspired and filled with hope by my students' resilience and their ability to learn, love, and laugh in the face of violence, misery, and despair.

My life story is a link in the chain connecting my great grandmother's, my grandmother's, and my mother's lived experiences. My educational endeavors and commitment to work that promote positive social and political change are possible because I am a product of their legacy. Generations of women in my family set an example for the strength of character and faith necessary to overcome adversity in a manner that serves not only the self and one's family, but also the broader community and society at large. I have a responsibility to live my life in a way that gives honor to so many sacrifices. I am called to tell our stories from a place of deep love and respect. This is not an easy prospect. Few things in my life have been easy. I am a Chicana.

Chapter 1: Familia

i write

i write because i live and love and hope
to heal old wounds

i write because it hurts
to carry generations of suffering
in my skin

i write because it helps me shed sorrow
layers of memory
i want to discard

i write because it is an act of courage
to look in the mirror,
see yourself naked,
and find the compassion
to touch every sore

i write to share my truths
because they are not just my own

i write to hear my voice
i write to forgive

i write because i hope
i write because i love

i write because i live

i live and love and hope because i write

escribo

escribo porque vivo y amo y tengo esperanza
de curar viejas heridas

escribo porque me duele
cargar con generaciones de sufrimiento
en la piel

escribo porque me ayuda a descartar tristezas
telas de memoria
que quiero desechar

escribo porque es un acto de valentía
mirar en el espejo
verse desnuda
y encontrar la compasión
para tocar cada llaga

escribo para compartir mis verdades
porque no sólo son mías

escribo para oír mi voz
escribo para perdonar

escribo porque tengo esperanza
escribo porque amo

escribo porque vivo

vivo y amo y tengo esperanza porque escribo

A Still Photograph of My Childhood

Every time I feel the row of acupuncture needles lining my back, my memory is flooded with rows of raisin grapes disappearing into the horizon. I often wonder, laying there on my tummy, my back and bottom exposed and vulnerable in the air-conditioned room of Dr. L's treatment room: in which of those rows did my body begin to deteriorate—years before I even entered puberty? I was a child, laboring like a man alongside my father in dusty rows of green, and purple, and brown. I was my father's shadow in those endless fields, making my body twist and lift, an impossible dance of rhythmic lifting, and bending, and dumping that would degenerate my bones and tear at my muscle tissue when I was supposed to be growing and developing into young womanhood.

I left my back in those seemingly endless rows of raisin grapes, laboring in the sweltering Central Valley heat to put food on our table, to help my family survive, while we put food on the tables of so many invisible faces. I often wonder who ate the raisins produced by the breaking of my back?

Dr. L's voice is gentle and empathetic as she struggles to push the needle into a particularly painful knot on the right side of my spine—tissue so long used to pain that it is tight and numb, and resistant to the relief the long, cold, pieces of metal are supposed to bring me. She repeats her litany every time my body resists the needle.

"Ooh, ooh, ooh..." she coos when a sharp stream of fire across my hip or down my leg causes me to jerk in pain.

"Oh, this is bad" she laments. "It is like trying to push a needle through a concrete slab. This pain in your back is so resistant. This section here, where it is the worst, in Chinese medicine we believe it is the section that holds childhood trauma. You have this. Trauma from childhood that is very old and very deep."

"I know." I mumble as the paper lining the table sticks to my face.

"How are you able to function every day with this kind of pain?" she asks me in exasperation. "Most of my patients with the level of pain I see in your back would be popping pills every moment."

"I don't know", I respond in between breaths, as I try to relax my body so she can continue.

"Usually people who have this level of pain are very grumpy, irritable, mean people because they are living with so much pain. Are you this kind of person?" I hear a smile in her voice when she asks the question.

I sigh a weak chuckle as I lay there half naked on her treatment table. "I try not to be, Dr. L. I guess I just learned to live with it. I honestly don't remember a time when my body wasn't in pain."

Dr. L connects several of the needles to a machine that will send electrical pulses into my back muscles through the needle points stuck in my tissue.

"Some of this pain is so deep", she tells me, "I am putting them several inches into your muscles and you barely flinch. This pain is very resistant."

As soon as she leaves me alone in the office to rest and let the needles do their magic, I begin to cry. Small sobs in between deep breaths because I need to lie still.

"Try to rest, Elvira", she whispered as she left the room. "Lie still and let the needles help you."

Those rows of raisins in the making always in the periphery of my emotional memory are now mimicked by the rows of needles marking ripples of pain imprinted on my body. In which of those rows did I leave my back? Did they all keep of piece of me? My childhood took place in those rows, surrounded by bunches and mounds of tiny purple bulbs of fruity sweetness, dried and shriveled into perfection by the same scorching sun rays that beat and burned onto and into my back. Dr. L tells me later that crying is a good side effect of some of the needles, and that it too will help me heal.

"We cannot fix you completely", she tells me, "but we can make it so you can feel better, and feel more free".

Every breath I take on that table, every needle into my spine, is a silent prayer. I don't want to be trapped in those fields any longer. God, help me let go of this pain. Help me heal my memory, my body, my back. I want to be free.

The Women I Come From

Recuerdo su cabello. Largo grueso y ondulado. Como el tuyo, mi'ja, pero completamente blanco. Por tantos años y una vida larga y dura. She took her time brushing her hair. Threading two long braids every day. *Tenía un cabello tan bonito.* I loved sitting with her when she brushed her hair. That is when she told us stories. *Nos platicaba de su vida. Nunca supo quienes fueron sus padres. Nadie sabe con seguridad. O quizás no quieren decir.* Her life was difficult. She raised her children on her own. *Si, ella solita creo a todos sus hijos y los hizo salir adelante.*

Mi abuelita Lolita. Your great-grandmother. The people who raised her may not have been her blood kin. Some say she was an "illegitimate" love child, given away by her mother — maybe a Tarahumara Indian. The Tarahumara are the tribal community closest to our ranchito in Mexico's northern state of Chihuahua. Others say that her mother was a victim of rape by the head of the house where she was hired as a servant. *Si, mija, en esos tiempos eso pasaba bien mucho.* This was a common fate for young women. *Mamá Lolita* was sent away to be raised by an uncle's family in order to keep the identity and virtue of her mother intact. She spent entire days *con su piernita* tied to a chair. *Para que no se saliera. Para que la gente no la viera.* Her family did not want her to go outside and be seen. She was supposed to remain invisible.

Lolita was married during her teen years. She birthed thirteen children. Her oldest son was in his teens, when her husband was murdered. He was herding cattle in the *sierra* and did not come home one night. *Mamá Lolita* sent the eldest boys to look for him. The family dogs led them to a cave. The boys found their father inside. He was slumped over against the earth with an ice pick hole in his neck. *Mamá Lolita* buried her husband and raised her children on her own. *Mis tios* always told me «*Doña Lolita era muy fuerte* ». She met her daughters' suitors at the door with a shotgun in her hands. *Los recibía con una carabina, por si acaso.* They say she never had to shoot, but she kept her family safe. I loved sitting with her when she brushed her hair. *Lo cepillaba con tanta ternura. Con tanta calma. Esas trenzas parecían lazos.* Every twist in her braids contained a story. *Cada nudo una memoria y yo me perdía en sus palabras.* Her words were magic. We must remember her stories and share them with our own children. These stories show us what we are made of. We are the courage and strength of the women we come from.

oldest brother

i was three years old
when i first remember meeting my oldest brother
and my maternal grandmother
we lived in Mexico
my father was in California
my father's family was supposed to take care of us
my grandmother knew she was dying
"i have come to return your son to you"
an older woman and a boy walked through the door
he was beautiful
i was awestruck
"this is your brother"
we played on the floor
toy cars raced on blue marble

my grandmother saw
that my father's sisters
did not know my mother had a son
she and my mother talked and cried all night
it was the first time she realized the extent
of my mother's suffering
grandmother wiped her tears on a tissue
they left the next day
my mother found the tear-stained tissue under a pillow
one month later grandmother died of a heart attack
my brother never came to live with us
my mother still keeps the tissue

hermano mayor

yo tenia tres años
la primera vez que conocí a mi hermano mayor
y a mi abuela materna
vivíamos en México
mi padre estaba en el norte
la familia de mi padre estaba supuesta a cuidarnos
mi abuela sabía que moriría pronto
«vengo a traerte a tu hijo»
una mujer mayor y un niño atravesaron la puerta
el era hermoso
yo estaba anonadada
«este es tu hermano»
jugamos en el piso
cochecitos corrían por el marfil azul

mi abuela se dio cuenta
que las cuñadas de mi padre
no sabían que mi madre tenía un hijo
las dos platicaron y lloraron toda la noche
fue la primera vez que ella supo
cuanto sufría mi madre
mi abuela se secó las lagrimas en un pañuelo de papel
se fueron el día siguiente
mi madre encontró el pañuelo debajo de una almohada
un mes después abuela murió de un paro cardiaco
mi hermano nunca vino a vivir con nosotros
mi madre aun guarda el pañuelo

for mario

for years i believed
you were only a whisper
a picture
a letter
a dream

in every reflection
of image and memory
there is a place in my story
where you should have been

for too long
i missed you
and hoped you were happy
away from our nightmares
my father
our pain

but each time i'm with you
and still feel the absence
i finally see it
i know it was wrong

in every reflection
of image and memory
there is a place in my story
where you should have been

despite the abuses
of tyrants and monsters
holding each other
we would have survived

you needed your mother
your sisters and brothers
to be more than a whisper
a picture

a letter
a dream

para mario

durante años creí
que tu eras solo un suspiro
un retrato
una carta
un sueño

en cada reflejo
de imagen y memoria
hay un lugar en mi historia
done debiste estar tu

por demasiado tiempo
te extrañé
y esperaba que fueras feliz
lejos de nuestras pesadillas
mi padre
nuestro dolor

pero cada vez que estoy contigo
y aun siento la ausencia
por fin me doy cuenta
que fue un error

en cada reflejo
de imagen y memoria
hay un lugar en mi historia
donde debiste estar tu

a pesar de abusos
de tiranos y monstruos
abrazados
hubiéramos sobrevivido

te hizo falta tu madre
tus hermanas y hermanos
debimos ser mas que un suspiro
un retrato

una carta
un sueño

Chapter 2: Schooling

El Bas

I hear the palote rolling onto the countertop as mami makes flour tortillas for breakfast. I wake to the smell of toasting flour and the sound of her voice.

«Hijos, ya es hora. Levántensen, o se les pasa el bas. »

We run to the bus stop most mornings, with a taco in hand. She will not let us leave for school without something warm in our bellies. *Aunque sea un taco.* Always a tortilla rolled with *papitas*, or *frijoles*, or butter or honey. *Pero aunque sea un taco.* We are the first picked up on the bus ride to our local public school. We need to get to the stop by 6:45am. We ride the bus for an hour around the rural route, on simple two-lane roads and some paths with barely enough concrete to keep the wide yellow bus off the dark earth that feeds the fields.

We drive by peach and plum orchards and fields of table, wine, and raisin grapes. I look out the bus windows, and often see my father working the fields of Mr. C's ranch on Lamar Avenue before we cross the narrow bridge into the part of the route that borders Reedley and Sanger. I see the top of his straw hat in one of the rows or his pickup parked on the side path that leads to the ranch house, and I am thankful that he does not make us work during day-school hours. The bus will pick up other farm workers' children as well as farmers' children. By the time we are in high school, the farmers' children will no longer ride the bus. Their parents will buy them cars, and they will drive themselves to school.

We sit in the back of the bus, trying to stay away from the bus driver's line of vision through the rearview mirror. He will be less likely to see us if we want to misbehave. The bus ride gives me a chance to talk with my friends before school. These are the "cool" seats because we can watch everyone else come on board. I get to see where the others live. I wonder about the big houses of the well-to-do children. Most of the other kids do not live in a mobile home like us. Even the kids I know, who work like we do, live in houses. Old houses, but houses nonetheless. Challo gets into a fight with some boys on the bus. They have been bothering me at school. The three boys are in third grade. All three are one year younger than Challo, and one year older than me. I punched one of them during recess yesterday. I warned him. I told him to stop singing that song.

"El-vira! El-vira! My heart's on fire for El-vira!"

He was chasing me around the playground singing that dumb song. So I finally got tired of it. I stopped and turned to face him. He charged towards me and before I knew what happened, he was lying on the ground, covering his face. We were in front of all the swing sets, full of girls swinging back and forth into the sky. The girls pointed and laughed at him. I walked away in a rush, feeling a lump of panic rise into my throat. I was terrified, but not of him. I was afraid of getting in trouble with the teacher on duty. If I get in trouble at school, it will be worse for me when I get home. He never tells on me.

On the bus, one of his buddies tries to trip me as I walk past their seat. Challo is walking behind me with his paper book bag in his arms. We carry our books to school in brown grocery bags because we cannot afford backpacks. One of the boys pokes me in the back with his finger and starts to say something, but Challo interrupts. My fists clench, and I can feel my body temperature begin to rise as Challo gets between us. The three boys stand up at the same time. Challo looks at me and says, "Get off the bus, Vira. Wait for me outside." I cannot hide the look of shock on my face. I have never seen my brother fight. He is quiet and gentle, and stays away from the other boys most of the time. My father constantly complains about what he perceives as Challo's lack of physical strength, and he makes comparisons between the two of us on a regular basis. «*No pareces mi hijo. ¿Cómo puede ser que tu hermana pueda más que tu?* » The boys turn to Challo, and I see him as my big brother for the first time. The bus driver does not stop them. He just laughs and lets them fight. Challo pushes one boy, and they topple over each other like dominoes. Then I see his right arm start swinging. And somehow he manages to hold onto his paper bag, clutching it with his left arm. I stand frozen, watching the scene unfold in sheer wonder. "Vira, get off the bus!" he repeats, and I wake from my reverie. He seems to have it under control, so I get off the bus and wait for him by the side of the road. He walks off in a few minutes. His face is red and his bag is ripped. He will have to ask *mami* for another paper bag. The bus driver is laughing to himself and shaking his head as the bus drives off. Challo takes my hand, and we walk together across the street, and onto the dirt path towards home. "Let's not tell *mami* what happened," he tells me. We will not get in trouble today. The boys never bother me again.

Kindergarten

It is my first day of school. *Mami* walks me to the classroom. The teacher introduces herself. She is Anglo and does not speak Spanish. I do not understand what she is saying. My stomach somersaults, and I feel the urge to run. The school secretary is bilingual and translates for my mother. They walk me to the playground, and I sit on a swing. It is a beautiful day. September in the Central Valley is warm and sunny. The grass is green, and the lawn is lush. Somebody must have watered the playground yard this morning. My father told me that without the water from the Sierra Nevada, this valley would be a desert, and the grass would be yellow and dry, like the hillsides. The fence around the playground is lined with broad-leafed trees. At home I would take my shoes off and run barefoot through the dirt and grass and climb at least one of the trees. But this playground is foreign territory, and I do not feel free. *Mami* told me I have to be a good girl and do what my teacher says. I sit by myself on the swing farthest from the rest of the girls. They speak English. I do not understand what they are saying. *Mami* turns to leave, and I want to call out to her, but I cannot allow the words to form. I hold them in my throat and choke back my fear. I want to be brave, like she asked, but I am not able to hold back my tears. I cry and swing and see the girls start to laugh and point at me. I look down at my *chanclas* through a waterfall of tears. White plastic slip-ons with the face of a brown teddy bear on the top. The teddy bear smiles up at me. Why are the girls laughing? My tears continue until the teacher walks over and takes my hand. She blows a whistle and calls out more words I do not understand. Everyone lines up, and we walk into the classroom. She shows me where to sit, on a small blue plastic-covered mat in the front half of the classroom. All the children have a mat, where we will nap after snack-time, or sit and listen while she reads us stories, or sing and chant when she talks about the letter people. *Mami* taught me *las vocales*, «ah, eh, ee, oh, oo » *y el abecedario* a long time ago. Now the teacher wants to show us the alphabet. I recognize the letters, but they sound different coming out of my teacher's mouth. In English, they are no longer warm and smooth, like my *mami's* voice. And the "*ll*", "*ñ*", and the "*ch*" are missing. But my teacher is nice, and *mami* told me to do what she says. «*La maestra sabe lo que les está enseñando* », she reminds us, «*ponle mucha atención, mija* ». I pay attention to the letter people sitting in the front of the class. They are funny looking and made of plastic. Blow-up dolls with bright colored limbs growing out of giant letter bodies. We take turns with a different letter every week. I memorize them all. Mr. M with a Munching Mouth. Mr. F with Funny Feet. Mr. T has Tall Teeth. At home, I practice words with my older brother.

«Challo, dime los colores. »

«Rojo es red. *Azul es* blue. *Amarillo es* yellow. »

«No, Challo. El hielo es blanco. ¿Cómo que, amarillo? »

«Si, Vira. Amarillo es yellow *y blanco es* white. »

«¡No, Challo! ¡El hielo es blanco, no amarillo! »

I argue back and forth with Challo until *mami* makes us stop. She will remind us every day for years to come: *«¡Ya, dejen su inglés para la escuela! Aquí solamente quiero oírlos hablar español. No quiero que se les olvide hablar como la gente. »*

elementary school

one hour bus ride
we were the first pick up
my brother, sister, and me
on the rural bus route
we were joined by our school mates
other farm worker's children, *mexicanos*, working-class, poor
farmer's children, caucasian, middle-class, rich
we sat at the back of the bus
coveted seats; furthest from the bus driver's watchful eye
one day the farmer's kids decided they wanted our seats
get out! wetbacks! go back to where you came from!

racistas pendejos, this is Aztlán

my father schooled us early about words meant to wound
wetbacks, greasers, beaners
don't let them make you think you are worth less
be proud of who you are!
don't pick fights, go to your teachers
my parents expected the best from our educators, respected their authority
confused, we went to the principal
mr. m, caucasian, middle-class, rich
he liked our family, we were good students
just ignore them, he advised
we listened, accepted ignorance
received good citizenship awards
a first step towards academic recognition
and future accomplishments

fourteen years later, at Stanford
trying to educate our classmates about farmworker civil rights
in the dark of the student theater, we were reminded
beaners, go home!
a community united
we could accept no more

racistas pendejos, this is Aztlán.

escuela primaria

una hora por autobús
nos recogían primero
a mi hermano, hermana, y a mí
en la ruta rural del autobús escolar
otros estudiantes viajaban con nosotros
otros hijos de campesinos, mexicanos, clase trabajadora, pobres
hijos de patrones, blancos, clase media, ricos
nos sentábamos en el asiento de atrás
asientos preferidos; los más alejados de la atenta mirada del conductor
un día los hijos de los patrones decidieron que querían nuestros asientos
¡fuera! ¡mojados! ¡regresen de donde vienen!

racistas pendejos, estamos en Aztlán

mi padre nos enseño acerca de las palabras dirigidas para herir
mojados, grasosos, frijoleros
no dejen que los hagan sentir que valen menos
¡sean orgullosos de lo que son!
no busquen pleitos, díganle a los maestros
mis padres esperaban lo mejor de nuestros maestros, respetaban su autoridad
confundidos fuimos con el director
el señor m., blanco, de clase media, rico
el apreciaba a nuestra familia, éramos buenos estudiantes
solo ignórenlos, nos aconsejó
hicimos caso, aceptamos la ignorancia
recibimos premios de buena conducta
un primer paso hacia el reconocimiento académico
y futuros logros

catorce años después, en Stanford
intentando educar a nuestros compañeros acerca de los derechos civiles de los campesinos
en la oscuridad del teatro estudiantil, nos recordaron
¡frijoleros, lárguense!
la comunidad se unió
no aceptaríamos más

racistas pendejos, estamos en Aztlán

Raising a Family

We are in and out of the hospital for six months. The hospital is in Fresno, a half hour drive from *la casita* in Reedley. *Mami* has to stay in the hospital many days at a time. I do not understand why she is so sick. Her asthma keeps getting worse. I am tired of the hospital. It smells of sterility and sadness. Every time we have to go back, I want to cry. *Pero quiero ver a mi mami.* I want to be close to her. I want her to hold me. The chairs in the emergency room are cold and uncomfortable. The plastic ridges around the seats dig into my back when I try to lie down across two chairs. So we sleep on the floor instead. The day the baby is born, my father takes us home from the hospital and asks:

«*Si pudieran tener otro hermanito, ¿qué prefirieran, un niño o una niña?* »

«*Un niño* », I say, anticipating what my father wants to hear.

He laughs. «*Que bueno porque les compramos un hermanito.* »

I am not able to sleep that night, trying to figure out where they found him. *¿Dónde se compran los niños?* We pick him up from the hospital on the following day. He looks nothing like I expected. Unlike the Gerber baby I have seen on television, our baby is brown, wrinkled and swollen at the same time. His face is swollen from all the medication *mami* had to take throughout the pregnancy. He almost didn't make it. *El bebe fue un milagro.* The pregnancy had been a secret my parents kept from everyone. *Mami* lost thirty pounds during the pregnancy. They did not even tell my godmother, *mami's* closest friend, who lives down the street from us. The doctors wanted *mami* to choose. They warned my father, «*la proxima vez se muere ella o el bebe.* » My father names the baby, Rómulo, his namesake. *Mami* gets sick again and has to go back to the hospital. My father has to return to the fields. The fruit ripens and will not wait for the family emergencies of laboring bodies.

«*Ya estas grande mija, tu tienes que cuidar a tus hermanitos.* »

«*Si apá, yo puedo.* »

I take care of the baby. He is my baby doll. He fits on my lap, and I rub his belly and sing him to sleep. « *A la ru ru niño, duérmeteme ya …* » I learn that to touch *con respeto* and *cariño* can comfort and heal. He is allergic to disposable diapers, so I learn to wash soiled cloths. Linda does not want him. She has been the baby for five years, and she doesn't want anyone to take her place. I have to negotiate time and attention between the two of them. He is smaller, and more helpless, so I have to protect him. Linda's wrath is the greater. I will be his shield for many years to come. We are all children after all, but I am the only one forced to play at being an adult. When *mami* comes home, she is still very sick, and weak. My new role as caretaker extends to her as well. I help count out her cocktail of pills. I can tell them apart by color, shape, and size. There are so many bottles. When I shake them, they sound like the baby's rattle.

«Mami, aquí está su medicina. »

I hand her each tablet and capsule, and I bring the glass of water to her mouth. I am six years old.

junior

i was six years old when my baby brother was born
my mother's asthma was chronic
she spent six months of her pregnancy hospitalized
my mother and father kept the secret
her doctors warned
she might have to choose
she prayed and tried to be patient
waiting for the baby
we lived in the hospital waiting room
little children trying to be patient
waiting for a baby we didn't know about
when they came home mother got sick again
back to the hospital
the baby stayed home
i was the big girl, so i took care of him
she came home still weak
i was the big girl, so i took care of her
i prayed and tried to be patient
i love my baby brother and my mother,
but i was thrilled when they grew up
and were able to take care of themselves

junior

yo tenía seis años cuando nació mi hermano menor
mi madre sufría de asma crónica
pasó seis meses de su embarazo hospitalizada
mi madre y padre guardaron el secreto
los doctores le advirtieron
quizás tendría que escoger
ella rezó y intentó ser paciente
esperando al bebé
vivíamos en la sala de espera
pequeñitos intentando ser paciente
esperando a un bebé del cual no sabíamos
cuando llegaron a casa mamá se enfermó de nuevo
de nuevo al hospital
el bebé se quedó en casa
yo era la mayor, así que me hice cargo de él
ella regresó a casa todavía débil
yo era la mayor, así que me hice cargo de ella
oré y traté de ser paciente
adoro a mi hermanito y a mi madre,
pero me dio muchísimo gusto cuando crecieron
y pudieron cuidar de sí mismos

En el Fil

I am dressed from head to toe in men's clothing. Layers cover every possible inch of skin in 115-degree weather. Sweat drips from each pore and muscle cells expand and contract with the ritual bending of my knees and back. I follow him down the row of grapes. I am my father's shadow in his old work shirt and pants. The vines are bursting with Johnson grapes, and we toil under the same sun that will dehydrate every bunch into raisins within a few days time. We are a team. He picks. I dump. I dance with my father down the row of grape vines, our movements choreographed in synch as we maximize time and motion. He moves down the row on his knees. We are both taller than the vines, and he must get under the blanket of foliage in order to reach each bunch of fruit. The dark green of the leaves is muted by a thin film of dust and chemical pesticides that attaches itself to our clothes, patches of exposed skin, inhaled with every breath. I am hunched over in a perpetual squat, my spine curves and hips swivel as I balance the tubs of fruit, one at a time. We exchange tubs of rusted metal, empty for full and full for empty. He fills a tub and puts it on the ground next to him. I give him my empty tub and lift the full one off the ground. I shift around in half a turn and dump the fruit over the brown sheets of paper that I first lay on the ground in front of me. This forward motion requires a delicate balance as I bend forward.

The farmer who hired us brought his tractor through each row before we started picking. He smoothed the earth with a flat metal disc so the grapes can dry on an even surface. I have to dump the fruit and spread it out on the paper without stepping forward. The paper needs to lie flat, so I must not step into the row and create uneven spots in the earth.

«*Si el patrón mira pisadas, se va a enojar,* » my father reminds me every day. «*Necesitamos el trabajo.* »

The sheet of paper is the color of a brown grocery bag and about three by four feet wide. Each paper is called a *tabla* because they used to be made out of wood. On a good day we get paid twelve cents per *tabla*, make two hundred *tablas* per row, and complete two rows. «*Mi hija trabaja como un hombre,* » my father boasts. «*Que lastima que naciste mujer.* » I am 12 years old.

survivors

i labored in the fields
cleaned other people's toilets
we had to survive
no matter how hot
or dirty

electricity rippled through my back
i had to prove i was just as strong
my brother couldn't compete
we both tried to be our father's son

my brother is gay
i am woman
such disappointments
we could never be
what my father wanted
so we gave up his dream
to follow our own
there is immense joy in freedom

sobrevivientes

laboraba en el campo
limpiaba baños ajenos
teníamos que sobrevivir
sin importar el calor
o la mugre

electricidad corría por mi espalda
tenia que demostrar la misma fuerza
mi hermano no podía competir
ambos tratamos ser el hijo de nuestro padre

mi hermano es gay
yo soy mujer
que descepciones
nunca pudimos ser
lo que mi padre queria
así es que dejamos su sueño
para seguir los nuestros
hay inmensa alegría en la libertad

challo

the big brother i grew up with
was always gentle, quiet, and misunderstood
not strong enough, or tough enough, for my father
he was my friend, and i tried to protect him
he beat up some boys once
who tried to bully me
i was very proud

in middle school he pulled me aside one day
would i still love him if he was gay

i made it my business to prepare our family
rented "Philadelphia", as a ploy
to bring up conversations
and let them know where i stood
in love and support
hoping they would someday understand

many years later, my brother officially came out
to me
to my family
a testimony of strength
i was very proud

challo

el hermano mayor con quien crecí
siempre fue amable, tranquilo, e incomprendido
no lo suficientemente duro o fuerte para mi padre
él era mi amigo, y yo traté de protegerlo
una vez golpeo unos muchachos
que quisieron molestarme
me sentí muy orgullosa

en la secundaria un día me preguntó
todavía lo querría si fuera gay

tome las riendas de preparar a la familia
rente "Philadelphia" como excusa
para empezar conversaciones
y dar a saber mi posición
en amor y apoyo
esperando que un día comprendieran

muchos años después, mi hermano se declaró
a mi
a mi familia
un testimonio de fuerza
me sentí muy orgullosa

Running and Waiting

My sophomore year in high school, I run cross-country with Linda and Challo. Practices are long and hard, especially at the beginning of the year, when the summer heat in Reedley has not tempered. It is dry and hot, and we practice, running up to 12 miles in the late afternoon, from 3:00 – 6:00 p.m. My parents are packing fruit this time of year, and they can only pick us up from practice after the sheds close. My siblings and I have worked in the same packing sheds with my parents until the first day of classes. Packing the last of the summer fruit: peaches, plums, and the first of the fall fruit: pomegranates and persimmons. Sometimes it gets really late because the fruit is ready, and they have to pack until the day's pick is finished. Today is one of those days. It is late, and we are hungry.

We shower in the school gym after practice and walk over to the convenience store on Manning and Reed, behind the high school and across the street from Reedley Community College. We rarely have any spending money. My earnings from cleaning the Ts' house are used for household expenses and some school supplies. We pool together our change and manage to scrounge up a dollar and fifty cents to buy a large drink and a small bowl of nachos. We share everything. This will have to hold us over until we get home. We walk back to school and wait. We wait in the school parking lot and watch the rest of the students drive away or get picked up. The last to go are the students who ride the late bus to Orange Cove, where the town is too small to have its own high school. We sit outside the gym and do our homework. I doubled up on math courses this year, taking both Geometry and Trigonometry because I want to take Calculus my senior year. My guidance counselor told me taking Calculus will make my college applications stronger. I have never even visited a college campus, but I believe it is the only way out of the fields and the sheds, so I will do what it takes to get there. Not doing my homework is not an option.

At 9:00 p.m. the school custodian asks us to leave the parking lot because he has to lock the school gate. His shift is over, and he needs to get home to his family. He says we can sit outside of the gate, on the sidewalk. We do as he says and sit on the curb to finish our homework, straining our eyesight under the street lamp. I am sore from practice and numb from sitting on the pavement with my back curved over my books. By the time my parents finally drive up, close to eleven o'clock and looking more exhausted than their children, I have finished my homework. We climb into the back of the yellow pickup and go home to get ready for another day. My senior year, a couple of middle-class Anglo males in my Calculus class will openly question why a Mexican girl got into Stanford University with a GPA slightly below a 4.0.

my face

freshman year in high school
the left side of my face was paralyzed
the doctor was stunned
you are so young
this usually happens to people in their twenties...

caused by excessive stress
movement should return in a few months
we were pruning vines that weekend
forced to leave early to take me to the emergency room
half a day's wages lost

first semester final exams started on monday
i went to school determined
i cried during my typing final
had to keep my fingers on the keys
my left eye couldn't blink
a lonely tear burned down my cheek
my teacher never noticed
i got an A in typing

mi cara

primer año de preparatoria
el lado izquierdo de mi cara quedo paralizado
el médico se sorprendió
eres tan joven
esto suele ocurrir a las personas en sus veinte años...

causado por el estrés excesivo
el movimiento debe regresar en unos meses
nos tocó podar viña ese fin de semana
obligados a salir temprano para llevarme a la sala de emergencia
perdimos la mitad del sueldo de un día

los exámenes finales del primer semestre empezaban el lunes
fui a la escuela con determinación
lloré durante mi examen de mecanografía
tuve que mantener mis dedos sobre las teclas
mi ojo izquierdo no podía parpadear
una lagrima solitaria quemó mi mejilla
el profesor nunca se dio cuenta
recibí un 10 en mecanografía

tears

as a child
my father taught me
crying was for the weak
he respected "strength"
my mother cried
he didn't respect her
i stood between them during fights
when i cried, my tears resolved nothing
he didn't stop
so i stopped
i willed back tears, relief, catharsis
pushed them back into my brain
my mind
my throat
compressing my lungs
pulsing back into my heart
muscles developed
as i struggled
to hold back tears
to be cool
to protect
so many cells wasted
trying to contain
my weakness

lagrimas

cuando niña
mi padre me enseño
que llorar era ser débil
él respetaba la "fuerza"
mí madre lloraba
él no la respetaba
me paraba en medio de ellos durante los pleitos
cuando yo lloraba, mis lagrimas no resolvían nada
él no se detenía
así es que yo me detuve
hice desaparecer mis lagrimas, el desahogo, la catarsis
las empuje hacia mi cerebro
mi mente
mi garganta
comprimiendo mis pulmones
pulsando dentro de mi corazón
desarrollé músculos
mientras luché
para detener lagrimas
para mantener la calma
para proteger
desperdicié demasiadas células
intentando contener
mi debilidad

Guadalajara

In Guadalajara, Jalisco, we live without a father. My father moves us there in the late nineteen seventies. He wants to live with his family and like his brothers, sell tacos in the city. He buys the cart, supplies, and starts the small business. Like my *tías* do for my *tíos*, my mother helps my father prepare the meat and condiments. She cooks the *carne*, chops the *cilantro, jitomates, y cebolla,* and makes the salsas. La *salsa verde de tomatillo y la roja de chile de arbol.* The weather is supposed to be better for my mother's chronic asthma. We left Reedley, California, where Challo, Linda, and I were born so our parents can give life in México another try. Within months, my father realizes he is not built for the city, or the business. He is from Las Animas, Zacatecas, *un ranchito,* and does not like his family's new urban lifestyle. «*Hay demasiada basura, cemento, ruido, y gente*», he complains. My father leaves us and moves back to Reedley. He promises to come back for us when he finds work and a place for us to live.

We stay in Guadalajara for nine months. The house we live in is my father's. He bought it with his savings from laboring in the fields in California for the past ten years. Two small bedrooms, a bathroom, and a kitchen surround a small patio with no ceiling. Cold hard blue and white marble covers the floors. I am overwhelmed by the artificial smell of pine cleaner, and I can see the sun's reflection in the tile after my mom finishes mopping. *Pero camino con cuidado porque si me resbalo de nuevo, esta vez me puedo romper el coco.* I do not worry about slipping and falling in the bathroom because the floor there is rough, bare cement and we have no plumbing, only a toilet that does not flush. The bowl does not have a water tank attached to it. We use buckets to pull water from a reservoir in the patio to pour into the toilet and drain it. We bathe in a large tin washtub with water drawn from the same reservoir.

My father's family is supposed to look out for us. One of my uncles moves into my father's house with his new bride. They take the bedroom next to the bathroom, and my mother, Challo, Linda, and I move into the smaller room facing the street. My *tía* claims the house as if it is her own. We are not her children, and she takes pleasure in yelling at us as she tries to discipline us.

¡No jueguen allí! ¡No hagan tanto ruido!

Linda and I suck our thumbs, and my *tía* is disgusted by our way of seeking comfort.

When my mother is not looking, she puts chile, petroleum, and who knows what else on our thumbs in her efforts to make us stop. My mother's asthma does not get better. The stress of our life in Guadalajara punishes her lungs. My father is away. My mother stays home to take care of us. Doña Rebeca lives across the street and tries to help. She offers my mother work threading leather belts to supplement the income my father sends from California. Challo and I also want to help. We spend hours threading leather belts, criss-crossing strings of leather into rows of parallel holes in each strap. Making crosses with our baby fingers. We do not have much to eat. My father is away. My *tía* gives us *pan dulce* one day, and we run to my mother excited about the treat. My mom takes it from us in tears and throws it out because it is stale and covered in mold.

Years later the same *tía* will come to California to live with us, and she will bring her three daughters with her. I will baby-sit them all. Feed and care for her children, as well as my siblings. In Guadalajara, my mother teaches me to write. I fill notebooks with my name. *Yo me llamo Elvira Prieto*. She teaches Challo and me to write, so we can send letters to my father. *Querido papi, venga por nosotros.* I am three years old.

La Mil Usos

The summer after seventh grade, I begin working for the Ts, a retired couple that lives across the street. He is a retired attorney, she a retired schoolteacher. They live in a large mission-style home that I become responsible for cleaning. The walls are built of thick adobe brick and the paneling on the windows and the massive double doors are made of fine dark wood. It is a beautiful home. I start out making minimum wage. I get paid $3.65 an hour to clean their toilets, help cook meals, bathe and care for their dogs and parrot, polish his shoes, work in their garden, help baby-sit their grandchildren, sweep, mop, vacuum, make beds, do laundry, and tutor him in Spanish. I learn to cook "American" meals and bake pastries while I help them prepare for the many dinner parties they host for their friends. I learn what it feels like to be invisible.

My parents have taught me to have manners and to show respect. *Yo soy bien educada.* I open the door for one of their guests on my way home after working several hours after school to make sure everything is ready for their bridge party. I smile at the couple cross-ing the patio's border, and I try to introduce myself. The old man looks away from me and walks past as if I am not there. He leaves me standing with my hand out in mid air. From then on I make sure to leave before any of the guests arrive. Mrs. T always lets me know afterwards how much her friends enjoy the food. She chuckles as she tells me that she let them believe she has done all the cooking herself.

Mr. and Mrs. T consider me an "exceptional young Mexican girl". They "just love" every-thing Mexico. They travel to Mexico at least once a year for a month at a time – to study the language, the food, and to paint. She paints in watercolor, and he works with oils. They encourage me to pursue a higher education. They buy me my first dictionary and thesaurus. They let me use their typewriter when I need to type reports for my Advanced Placement English, History, and Government classes. I work for them until I finish high school and leave for Stanford. They give me a raise when minimum wage increases to $4.25 an hour.

I work for the Ts after school and on weekends. I work for them because I do not have much of a choice. We live in the rural part of my hometown, and I do not have trans-portation for minimum wage at the few fast food restaurants in town. It is my first real paycheck. I have worked in the fields alongside my parents since I was six or seven, but my labor has been included in my parents' pay. To work for the T's, all I have to do is walk across the street. I cross that street day after day because I need the money. My family needs the money. There are days when I work in the fields with my family from sun-up until around 4:30 p.m. when our bodies can no longer stand in the sweltering summer heat. I go home to shower and have a quick supper before heading over to the Ts for another three to four hours. Working for the Ts, I test the limits of my physical endurance and my capacity for patience. I am exhausted.

Chapter 3: Life and Violence

unforgettable

it was like a topographical map of my home state
mountain ranges, valleys, and vast bodies of water
beautiful hues of green, on purple, on blue

i was shocked by their richness
so unnatural against the paleness of the canvas

i couldn't stop staring
mystified by the source of such artistry

i could feel it's throbbing heat
recoil at my touch
my own pulse quickened to match

i will never forget the landscape
the bloom of colors
my father's boots painted
on my mother's skin

inolvidable

parecía un mapa topográfico de mi estado natal
cordilleras, valles y vastos cuerpos de agua
hermosos colores verde, púrpura y azul

me estremeció su riqueza
tan antinatural en contrasto con la palidez del lienzo

no pude despegar la mirada
mistificada por la fuente del arte

brincó cuando la toque
podía sentir su palpitante calor
mi propio pulso aceleró a su compás

nunca olvidare el paisaje
el brote de colores
que pintaron las botas de mi padre
en la piel de mi madre

bruises

i remember screams
go outside!
he ordered
sweep off the fence!
we knew he was going to hit her
stop crying and do what I say!
doors slammed
my mother screamed
my father cursed
she begged for mercy
¡por favor, por mis hijos!
he cursed
apparently we weren't worth much
he beat her with an extension cord, belt, cowboy boots
he sent us out because he didn't want us to see
he forgot the three-year-old crouching in the corner
i screamed, raged, hated him
swore when i was big enough i would hurt him
i wanted to be a big man, so i could protect my mom
i beat the fence with all the force i had
i screamed, i cried
that was all i could do
and hit the broom against the fence
my father beat my mother until he was spent
i let the broom fall, exhausted
her blue, green, purple bruises took weeks to heal
mine do not have colors
but they are still there

moretes

recuerdo gritos
¡salgan para afuera!
nos ordenaba
¡ponganse a barrir el corral!
sabíamos que le iba a pegar
¡no chillen! ¡hagan lo que les digo!
las puertas tranqueaban
mi madre gritaba
mi padre maldecía
ella pedía misericordia
¡por favor, por mis hijos!
el maldecía
parece que no valíamos mucho
el le pego con una extensión, un cinto, botas vaqueras
nos mando para fuera por que no quería testigos
el niño de tres años estuvo presente
yo gritaba, llena de rabia, lo odiaba
juré que cuando grande le haría daño
yo quería ser hombre grande para proteger a mi mama
yo le di a el corral con todas mis fuerzas
grité, lloré
era lo única que podía hacer
y golpear la escoba contra el corral
mí padre golpeo a mi madre hasta cansarse
yo deje caer la escoba, agotada
sus moretes azul, verde, púrpura duraron semanas para sanar
los míos no son de colores
pero todavía los siento

love and marriage

i split them up
my father went outside
i followed him, trying to mediate
the sun was setting over the grape fields
red, purple, green tangles of sky, fruit, and vine

i sat next to him on the yellow steps
several shades brighter than our mobile home
i helped build and paint them years before

tired of breaking up fights
i wanted to understand the source of their rage

dad, didn't you love mami when you got married?
he looked towards the horizon
no.
my heart fell to the earth and rolled under the steps
then why did you get together with her?
i followed his gaze
i was just having fun, i didn't plan on marrying her

the sky darkened before my eyes
i refused to cry in his presence
he valued emotional strength
i wanted to please him

i asked my mother the same questions
i wanted a father for my son

no love?
what did that say about me?
i was their child
they had no business answering my questions

it took me twenty years to understand
i could be born into love
even when conceived without it

amor y matrimonio

los separé
mi padre salió
lo seguí, intentando mediar
el sol bajaba sobre los campos de uva
rojo, púrpura y verdes varañas de cielo, fruta y viña

me senté junto a el en los escalones amarillos
varios tonos más brillantes que nuestra traila
ayude a construir y pintarlos años antes

cansada de parar sus pleitos
quería entender la fuente de su ira

apá, ¿que usted no quería a mami cuando se casaron?
el miró hacia el horizonte
no.
mi corazón cayó a la tierra y rodó debajo de los escalones
entonces ¿po rqué se junto con ella?
seguí su mirada
solo me divertía, no pensaba casarme con ella

el cielo se oscureció ante mis ojos
me negué a llorar en su presencia
el valoraba la fuerza emocional
yo quería complacerlo

le hice las mismas preguntas a mi madre
yo quería un padre para mi hijo

¿sin amor?
¿qué decía eso de mí?
yo era su hija
no debieron responder a mis preguntas

me tomó veinte años para entender
que pude nacer en el amor
incluso cuando concebida sin el

Como Sobrevivir

I walk through the sliding glass door in the rear of the mobile home and descend the yellow staircase into the graying afternoon. It is late in the day, and the sun is setting over the grapefruit trees by the street across the front yard. The walnut trees behind the mobile home create a natural canopy of shade during the hot summer months. My father has called us all outside. He pulls a couple of rabbits from their pens. We have grown up with pigs, goats, chickens, rabbits, and an occasional calf in pens and coops behind our mobile home. We help my father build the pens and coops for all of the animals. We raise our animals for consumption because my father believes it is healthier for us to eat fresh, home grown meat. And it is more cost-effective than store-bought when you can raise the animals *en el rancho*. We do not have to buy all of their feed. There is plenty of grass to cut and leftover fruit from the vineyards and orchards.

Mami, Linda, and Challo usually care for the animals while I work inside. The household chores are mine. Cleaning, cooking, feeding. Challo and Linda help outside with the animals. They help *mami* with the slaughtering. I do not mind eating the fresh meat; this is how I have grown up. But the slaughtering is another story. It makes me sad. I usually hide in the bedroom and cover my face with a pillow when I know they are going to kill one of the larger animals. Especially when it is one of the pigs. They sound like people. The gunshot reverberates in my brain, and the inevitable chorus of diminishing squeals follows. There are times when I watch my father and my *nino* cut up the carcass afterwards, fascinated by the careful steps they follow: washing, shaving, skinning, carving. I pay attention and the skilled labor I witness comes in handy during seventh grade biology. My dissection of the frog and guinea pig will be the best in my class. Neat incisions with all the organs carefully separated and identified. My teacher will marvel at the steadiness of my hand, and the ability to concentrate, while a couple of the boys in my class throw mashed brains at each other at the desk next to me. *No tienen respeto*. The poor animals are already dead. I do the assignment well and with respect. Ultimately, I can handle the presence of the carcass, but I have never been able to deal with the moment of death. Today, my father wants me to learn how to kill.

I try to be strong. «*No apá, no puedo.*»

«*¿Cómo que no? Ándale, tienes que aprender. ¿Qué tal que un día se te ofrece tener que matar un animal? Tienes que saber como sobrevivir. ¿Apoco, por cobarde, te vas a morir de hambre?*»

I feel tears roll down my face. «*¡No!*» I argue. «*¡Prefiero comer zacate!*»

«*¡Ándale, ya dije!*» He is already angry. «*Pareces niña chiquita.*»

«*Apá, no puedo.*»

Linda and Challo stand by and watch. They are scared. I am alone.

«*Vente mija,*» my mother tells me. «*Yo te ayudo. Tu nomas lo detienes.*»

«*¡Ándale!*» I know the finality of my father's tone well. I am defeated.

Mami hangs the rabbit by its hind feet on the rusted metal bar of the old swing set. She hands me the front legs and tells me to hold the head back. I hold the front legs together with my left hand and the head with my right. I am sobbing uncontrollably now, and I can feel the rabbit shaking with me. *Mami* takes the knife and cuts at the throat with a quick thrust. The knife is not as sharp as she expected, and she has to make several attempts.

«*Ay Dios mío este cuchillo no tiene suficiente filo,*» she says, and I see tears running down her own cheeks.

I can feel its throat pulsing in my hand as it struggles to swallow and breathe. She finally makes the fatal slice, and the rabbit dies in my hands. I feel the last shudder of warmth released from the small body, as blood pools on the gray earth under my feet. Mami looks at me. «*Ya mija, ya pasó.*» I cannot stop shaking and crying. I look at my father, and he turns away from me. He walks off, disappointed at my weakness, while my mother and Challo finish skinning the soft brown fur. I am 16 years old.

her heart

my mom has chronic asthma
when i was a child
her heart stopped
i waited with her for my father to come home
her attack started an hour earlier
he was drinking with my uncle
she didn't want to call an ambulance
we couldn't afford
i sat with her on the steps of our mobile home
rubbed her back, willing my father to come home
i was furious and terrified when he finally arrived
i climbed in the pickup
the hospital was thirty minutes away
he sped
she vomited in my lap, collapsed
she felt heavy against my shoulder, passed out
my father drove into the emergency driveway
i ran into the hospital
he carried her in behind me
"my wife has asthma", he croaked, his accent thick
i had never seen him so frightened
my mom lay on a gurney
as the receptionist asked for insurance information
"please, my wife has asthma"
an ER doctor came out, took pity
they wheeled her away
we sat in the waiting room
it felt like forever
when they finally let us see her
she had tubes coming out of her mouth, her arms
and wires taped to her chest
the doctor was serious when he told us
"her heart stopped
five minutes later, we couldn't have brought her back"

su corazón

mi madre tiene asma crónica
cuando yo era niña
su corazón paró
espere con ella para que llegara mi padre
el ataque empezó una hora antes
mi padre estaba tomanbo con mi tío
ella no quería llamar a una ambulancia
que no podíamos pagar
yo espere con ella en los escalones de nuestra traila
le sobe la espalda, rogando que mi padre llegara pronto
estaba furiosa y aterrorizada cuando finalmente llegó
subí a la camioneta
el hospital quedaba a treinta minutos de camino
volábamos por la carretera
ella se vomitó en mi regazo y se desmayó
se sentía pesada contra mi hombro, desvanecida
mi padre condujo hasta la entrada de emergencia
yo corrí a el hospital
el la cargaba tras de mi
«mi esposa tiene asma», gritó, su acento grueso
nunca lo había visto tan asustado
mi madre yacía en una camilla
la recepcionista nos pedía seguro médico
«por favor, mi esposa tiene asma»
un doctor salió, nos tuvo lástima
se la llevaron
nos sentamos en la sala de espera
parecía una eternidad
cuando finalmente nos dejaron verla
tenía tubos por la boca, en sus brazos
y cables pegados al pecho
el doctor se acercó muy serio
«su corazón paró
cinco minutos más tarde, no hubiera vuelto»

woman

wise beyond her years
an old woman looking through the eyes of a baby girl
the first time she was molested
the first time she was told she was ugly
the first time she tasted fear
the first time she felt alone
she thought she deserved hell
in his rage, her father cursed her
i hope you find a man who will put you in your place
you need to be taught what it means to be a woman
too late

mujer

sabia mas allá de su edad
una anciana mirando a tráves de los ojos de una niña
la primera vez que abusaron de ella sexualmente
la primera vez que la llamaron fea
la primera vez que probó el miedo
la primera vez que se sintió sola
pensó que merecía el infierno
en su rabia, su padre la maldijo
ojala y te toque un hombre que te ponga en tu lugar
necesitas que te enseñen lo que es ser mujer
ya era demasiado tarde

La Casita Blanca

I am four years old when my father brings us back from Guadalajara, and we move into *la casita blanca.* The wooden house is old, and we will be forced to leave it in five years time. It will be condemned as dilapidated and inhospitable for human dwelling. The walls bare witness to unspeakable violence, abuse, and loss. *La casita* will be demolished, and the walls will crumble, unable to carry the burden of so much life. And death. *La casita* bore my creation stories. The creation of my motherhood necessitated the dissolution of my childhood. The loss of my innocence. I learned to take care of others, to put their needs first. I took care of babies. I took care of grown-ups. I helped potty-train Linda. She is one year and five months younger than me. I was a buffer. I turned my body into a shield. I protected my sister. I defended my mother. I raised my brothers. I sat with my father and his brothers while they attempted to drink away hardships, struggle, and pain. I learned to mix their drinks. Soda and whiskey, or rum, or brandy, or whatever else was on sale.

«Ponle dos hielos a cada vaso, mija. Tres dedos de pisto, y tres de soda.»

I collected the empty frosted brown barrilitos of cheap Lucky beer. The men drank and sang, and I became their *segunda voz. Me desvelaba con ellos,* and I watched them drink until their bodies were saturated and forced to regurgitate into unconsciousness. I cleaned up their vomit. I wiped the poison from their faces, their clothes, and mopped it up off the floor. I held my breath. My father wanted me to be his son. My mother wanted me to be her friend. *Hija de nadie.* I learned to fight for others. I took the burdens from the walls and built my armor, from splinters and chards. I developed muscles to carry those stories. To carry my shame. Hell was a certainty. I was caught *en las llamas* and was almost engulfed. In order to escape the circle of flames, I had to give up my soul. *En la casita*, I conquered my fear of the dark. I could no longer be a little girl.

***

When we first move back from Mexico, *vivimos en la casita blanca*, across the street from my madrina's house on Crawford Avenue. *La casita blanca*, is one of many places we will live before I finish school. *La casita tiene una recamara, una sala,* a kitchen and a small dining room. Its walls are made of wood and plaster, and my father and his brothers painted the wood paneling on the outside with cheap white paint to try to camouflage its age. *Mami y apa duermen en el cuarto de enfrente.* Their bedroom door is closest to the front door, on the immediate left of *la casita's* front entrance. The front door is made of wood, chipped and splintering with year's of exposure to the extreme weather of the Central Valley. The summer sun scorches the simple wooden structure and the freezing winter fogs fill its crevices with mold. The floors are covered in fading yellow linoleum, and I hear the floorboards creak as I walk from room to room. My favorite room is *la sala*, because *mami* covers its walls with our completed homework sheets and ripped out pages of the coloring books I love to fill. She creates *rascuache* wallpaper out of our elementary school achievements, artwork, and the homework papers covered in our baby handwriting and some of the highest scores in our grade levels. Mi mama celebrates our accomplishments in whatever way she can.

«*Me encante ver sus tareas, mis hijos. Todos tienen tan buenas marcas. Mira que bonitas se ven las paredes con su trabajo.*»

My siblings and I sleep in a bedroom with many doorways but no doors. It is a small space connected to the living room on the eastside of the house, the same side facing away from the front door. This room may have once been a dining room that was turned into a bedroom for us to share. The kitchen is connected to our bedroom on the south side of the house and to the one bathroom we all share on the north. Next door to us on the west side of the house is an outside room, something attached to the house many years after it was originally built. This room is ugly and distorted, like a tumor growing out of the houses' back. We call it *el cuartito*. This is where my uncles stay when they come from Mexico for periods of time to work in the fields with my family. They live with us several months at a time following the prep and picking season of several varieties of fruit. *Se la pasan piscando durazno y ciruela al principio de la primavera* and often stay to pick grapes in the late summer or to prune vines in the winter. This is the same room where one of my uncles and his family will stay when they first arrive from Mexico. My *tío* J, his wife, and their three oldest daughters will live in *el cuartito, en la casita con nosotros* several years from now. The uncles that stay with us in *el cuartito* are my father's younger brothers. The only family that stays with us, and for whom my mother always cooks and cleans, is my father's family.

It is early evening and the sun is gone, set into the far western horizon, rich hues of orange and blood red over the miles of dark green vineyards covering the earth. My mom, dad, and *tío* J aren't home. I don't know where they went. I don't remember if they told me. I am four year's old, Linda is three, and Challo is six.

¿Dónde esta Challo?

When he isn't doing chores, feeding or herding the animals my father keeps for our consumption, my brother often hides out, staying away from my father's wrath. *Mi apa siempre dice que Challo no es fuerte.* He often makes us fight each other, play boxing, to test our strength. I always try to impress my father by hitting my big brother with all my strength, while my father and uncles laugh and call out punches. Mi father's voice rings out with rage.

«¡Muchacho cabron! ¿Cómo es posible que tu hermana pueda más que tu?»

He is always comparing us and readily tells me how much he wishes I was born a boy. I should have been the son he wants. According to my father, my strength is a waste.

«Es una lastima que haigas nacido mujer.»

Linda and I are wearing our pajamas, *batitas largas,* made of soft flowered but faded cotton, with a ruffle trim along the hem. I think they came in the cardboard box of clothes my nina brought over from her house. *La ropa* that her girls don't need or like anymore. I always get so excited when she brings us boxes of hand me downs because the clothes are new to us, and my mom always mends them to fit our younger bodies.

I hear my tio's voice calling from *el cuartito.* This man is one of my father's brothers who is also younger than my tío J. I don't remember what he says to us. Why is it so hard to remember? How did he call us into the room? I go to him because I want attention, *cariño,* love. I know I am supposed to do what grownups tell me to do. The litany of my father's *verdades* echoes in every cell of my baby body.

«Hazle caso a tus mayores, mija, especialmente a tu familia.»

«Los hombres siempre son mejores que las mujeres.»

«Las mujeres nacieron para servirnos a los hombres.»

«Yo soy su padre. Mi esposa y mis hijos son míos. Me pertenecen.»

«Yo puedo hacer lo que me de la gana con ustedes.»

«Más les vale obedecer.»

«Yo soy el hombre, y soy el que mando aquí.»

«Nadie te va a cuidar ni a proteger en este mundo como lo hace tu padre.»

I often share my father's wish that I was born a boy. I want to be like my father. I want to do as I please. I want to be free.

My uncle's voice is tender and full of playful pleading.

«Ven para acá mija, acuéstate conmigo.»

He lightly pats the blanket folded on the floor next to him. Linda follows me into *el cuartito*. My baby sister always wants to be where I am, to go where I go. *El cuartito* is full of dark shadows, with light streaming in from its only window facing the west side of the house. The walls are thin planks of bare brown wood, some partially covered in yellowing plaster board that was once white. Several years from now, when our extended family no longer stays with us, *el cuartito* will become our playroom. This will be the room where my siblings and I can escape during the cherished moments when we play together and live out the adventures of our childhood fantasies. *El cuartito* is small, with a low ceiling. The weather and elements affect this space more than the rest of the house. The heat in this ten by ten foot space always feels hotter and the cold more achingly frozen than in the rest of *la casita*.

I lie down next to him and keep Linda on the other side, away from my uncle. I am a curious, sad little girl, and I have already been trained to take care of others, to please them.

«Las mujeres deben de servir a los hombres.»

«Las mujeres y los niños siempre tienen que obedecer.»

My *tío* puts his hands on me. He lifts my *batita* and looks at my body. He touches me, and he touches himself. He leads my hands onto his body, showing me what he wants me to do. His skin is rough, dark and calloused from hours of laboring in dirt and sun. His breath is close to my face, hot and sour like my father's after he drinks his daily *cerveza* or *trago* of hard liquor and cola.

«Tres dedos de pisto y tres de soda, mi'ja.»

My dad taught me how to mix his drinks a long time ago. The grown men in my family always have alcohol on their breath.

My father's brother tells me to touch him. I do as he says. It doesn't feel good. His skin is hot and sweaty. Something is wrong. He wants me to kiss him there. It is big and swollen. He asks me to kiss it again. The musty scent of over-ripened fruit in the fields surrounds me. The dust and mold in the walls of *el cuartito* fill my lungs. I am enveloped in sulfur, chemical pesticides, sweat and earth. These smells will shock my body into violent memories at every entrance into the Central Valley for the rest of my life. Stomach churning memories of my childhood are triggered by the vision of brown male bodies arched away from the sun and will forever fill the valleys of my home. A home I will take with me like a turtle, every wound, *cada recuerdo*, forming a heavy ragged shell to carry on my back.

«Tienes que hacerle caso a tus mayores, mija. Especialmente a tu familia.»

«Los hombres mandan y las mujeres deben obedecer.»

The musky scent of his manhood, the deep brown rough texture of his skin becomes embedded in every cell of my body. *No me gusta. Pero a el si le gusta*, so I continue to do what he wants.

«Así mija.»

He moans and sighs. Then his voice becomes rushed and harsh.

«No le vallas a decir a tu papá porque se va a enojar contigo y después te pega.»

Me siento mal, sucia, my memory becomes fuzzy. Is Linda still next to me? *¿Puede ver mi hermanita lo que esta pasando?* Why does he want me to do this? I thought he was going to tell us a story, *un cuento*, like mami does and then hold us until we fell asleep. *Mi mami siempre nos murmura cuentos de aventura y amor antes de dormir.* She taught us how to say our prayers, and then she always gives us her blessing before we go to sleep.

«Que sueñen con los angelitos, mis hijas.»

I don't know if Linda can see what I am doing, what is happening to me. I never ask her, but I hope she doesn't see. I hope she will never remember this moment, or any others. I am suffocated by the bed sheets covering the top of my head, my shoulders, as he repeats his murmurs and grunts.

«No le vayas a decir a tu papá lo que estamos haciendo, mija. Si le dices no te va a creer. Nomas se va a enojar y te va a pegar.»

I don't know how long we lay there with him. *Que tanto más paso*. I am jolted and pushed away from his body when I hear the front door open and my father rushes in with mami and my *tío* J on his trail.

«¿Qué están haciendo con su tío?» my father booms across the sala into the hallway.

«Nada, apá.» I say echoing my uncle's hurried response.

I am confused and terrified. I feel ugly and rotten for telling a lie, but I don't want my father to get mad. My throat is dry, and I want to throw up. When mi apá gets mad, he hurts my mom. I will do anything to keep him from hurting my mother.

«¿Que estaban haciendo en al cuartito con su tío?»

My baby sister stands next to me, silent. My heart is going to burst out of my chest.

«Nada, apá.»

«Bueno, ya acuéstense a dormir,» my father commands, and Linda and I crawl into the bed we share on one side of our room.

The small twin bed we share is pushed against the wall next to the doorway that leads into the living room. The bed frame is made of cold metal covered in red paint peeling off the springs that hold up our small mattress. The bed was used and old when *mami* and *papi* brought it for us. The metal creaks and screeches under our shared weight. The doorway to *el cuartito* is next to the bed where Challo sleeps. Challo is still not here. He must be outside, checking on the animals or bringing the chickens into the pen where they sleep at night. My father makes sure we keep the animals safe and away from the many predators who would destroy or consume them during the night. My sister wraps her baby arms around me, and we cuddle together *en la camita* as I tremble, my body shivering and cold. *Tengo tanto miedo.*

Me siento sucia, pecadora, y estoy segura que voy a ir al infierno por lo que me paso. I pray to *la Virgencita* every night for forgiveness. This is a prayer I will repeat for years to come. I pray feverishly, always certain I am ugly and despicable, and I deserve to go to hell.

«Dios te salve María.
Llena eres de gracia.
El Señor es contigo.
Bendita tu eres entre todas la mujeres.

Y bendito es el fruto de tu vientre, Jesús.»

Twelve years will pass before I tell my parents the truth. Together with Challo, my beautiful and gentle older brother, who has a similar and yet more horrifying truth to tell about more than one of my father's brothers. My father receives the news in shock and exasperation. His voice cracks with pain and rage.

«*¿Cómo es posible? ¿Por qué no me dijieron?*»

«*Porque teníamos miedo, apa.*»

He can't believe we waited so long to tell him. And yet, our truth seems to make no difference. Our pain, our *recuerdos*, do not visibly change my father's relationship to his brother. As far as I know he never even addresses the issue with him. More than thirty years later, when his brother succumbs to complications resulting from alcoholism and diabetes, my father will cry with grief at the loss of his brother. He will travel to Mexico to be with his family, to share in their pain and mourn his brother's death.

Hasta el final, siento que mi papá lo escoge a el, a su hermano, como a su hermana, y a su mamá. Ellos son su familia, y siempre los pondrá antes que a nosotros. After all, we were just his property, his children and his wife.

i wish you hadn't said

you're just a girl
men are stronger
women do what men say
don't cry
don't get mad
don't talk back

i don't want you to look like me because i am ugly
you're too fat
your sister has lighter skin, straighter hair
her name means beautiful, you know
don't cry
don't get mad
don't talk back

do what I say
don't tell anyone our secrets
nobody will believe you
don't cry
don't get mad
don't talk back

get your father's permission
of course you got straight As, you are my daughter
you need to be a big girl
don't cry
don't get mad
don't talk back

wetbacks! go back to where you came from!
you will never get into Stanford
you only got into Stanford because you are a woman of color
don't cry
don't get mad
don't talk back

you are so big and strong – you should have been born a man
you are no longer my daughter

don't cry
don't get mad
don't talk back

you don't look mexican...
what are you?
if only you were thinner, you could be beautiful
don't cry
don't get mad
don't talk back

i wish you hadn't said

afraid to disappoint you
i choked back tears
swallowed contradictions
don't cry
don't get mad
don't talk back

i was determined to survive your words
bony dermal plates of turtle shell
every phrase a layer of armor
i carried on my back
don't cry
don't get mad
don't talk back

i would accomplish as much as any man
confusing martyrdom for strength
neglected my womanhood
don't cry
don't get mad
don't talk back

thank God i woke up to myself
everything you said was wrong
you will hear me
cry, get mad
and never stop talking back

quisiera que nunca me hubieras dicho

solo eres niña
los hombres son más fuertes
las mujeres hacen lo que los hombres dicen
no llores
no te enojes
no rezongues

no quiero que te parezcas a mi porque yo soy fea
estas muy gorda
tu hermana es más blanca, tiene el pelo lacio
su nombre significa bonita, sabes
no llores
no te enojes
no rezongues

haz lo que te digo
no le digas nuestros secretos a nadie
nadie te va a creer
no llores
no te enojes
no rezongues

pídele permiso a tu papá
claro que recibiste puras As, eres mi hija
tienes que comportarte como señorita
no llores
no te enojes
no rezongues

¡mojados! ¡regresen de donde vinieron!
nunca te aceptarán a Stanford
te aceptaron a Stanford solo porque eres mujer de color
no llores
no te enojes
no rezongues

eres tan grandota y fuerte – que lastima que no naciste hombre
ya no eres mi hija

no llores
no te enojes
no rezongues

no pareces mexicana...
¿qué eres?
si fueras más delgada, podrías ser bella
no llores
no te enojes
no rezongues

quisiera que nunca me hubieras dicho

temí decepcionarte
ahogué mis lagrimas
tragué contradicciones
no llores
no te enojes
no rezongues

determinada a sobrevivir tus palabras
óseos platos de concha de tortuga
cada frase una capa de armadura
que cargué sobre mi espalda
no llores
no te enojes
no rezongues

lograría tanto como cualquier hombre
confundiendo el martirio con la fuerza
descuidé mi condición femenina
no llores
no te enojes
no rezongues

gracias a Dios me desperté
todo lo que me dijiste fue falso
ahora tendrás que escucharme
llorar, enojarme
y nunca dejaré de rezongar

pintura de arena

también los llevo en mi cuerpo
pero por dentro
donde no tan facil se pueden ver

o quizas, sí

maybe you can see my bruises
depending on the angle
in which you look at me

los llevo como carga
en mis pulmones
cuando no puedo respirar

son bolsas de arena
taken from the beaches
of my mother's skin
donde las imagenes de tierra
hacian frontera contra el mar

cada recuerdo de violencia
llena mi interior
blocking my airwaves
crushing my heart

mi corazón esta rasgado
de tantas rupturas

every bruise on my mother's body
is reflected in my core

el mapa corre por mi columna
freeways branching out
en discos desgastados
por tanto trabajo
por querer demostrar
que yo
una niña

podia trabajar en el campo
como hombre

mi mapa es todo un mundo
de tierra y mar interno
y la concha de tortugá
que llevo en la espalda

my invisible turtle shell is my home
every memory
a bony dermal plate
i carry on my back

sí, mis moretes estan aquí
siempre
and they may never disappear

I Love my Father

Sí, yo amo a mi padre. Por darme vida. Por no sacarme de la escuela. For working his ass off so we could have food in our bellies. For coming back each time he was deported. Crossing the river, the sierra, so many borders. He almost died. But he kept coming back to be with us. *Quería cuidar a su familia.* The way his own father taught him.

Sí, yo se que en su propia manera el me ama. Pero tengo tanto sentimiento, so much anger.

Sabes yo queria ser come el when I was little. Lo recuerdo como un sueño. I thought my father was beautiful. *Un hombre grande y fuerte. Y tan guapo.* I wanted to look like him. To grow up to be just like *mi apá. Pero ese sueño fue muy corto.*

¿Cuándo desperte?

La primera vez que me di cuenta. The first time I saw him hit my mom. *Con palabras de ira. Tanto coraje sin sentido. Y luego los moretones en la piel de mi mamá.* The bruises on my mother's body *parecian un mapa. Tu sabes. Asi con* landscapes *de muchos colores.* Topographical maps where you see browns and greens and blues. *Para que sepas donde termina la tierra y donde comienza el mar.*

That's how her skin looked. Those bruises took weeks to heal. *Con el tiempo las marcas se hacian mas chicas.* Like the land was shrinking. And getting darker. They got black over time. Shrinking into small specks. *Hasta que se desaparecían.*

Until the next time. Until I was big enough to make him stop.

When did it start? *Pues desde antes que yo naciera.*

You know, Challo was born with a birthmark. *Sí. En su cadera.* He was born with his own small map on the back of his newborn hips.

My dad came home from the cantina with hickies and lipstick on his neck.

My mom questioned him.

La verdad no se porque. She could see him from the kitchen window. *La cantina estaba al cruzar la calle. Allí por la esquina de la Crawford y la Adams. Dice mi ama que se llamaba "El Flamingo". Pues ahí.* She could see him from the window of her kitchen, drinking and dancing *con todas las cantineras.*

Pues, esa noche, 8 months pregnant with Challo, *mi amá le reclamo a mi apa sobre los* hickeys and the lipstick. I can imagine my father, stumbling into the kitchen, drunk and reeking of alcohol and cheap perfume. *Pues a mi me toco verlo haci tantas veces despues.*

Pero cuando su mujer, his property, had the nerve to question him, *el se llenó de rabia y la sacó con ella. Le pegó y la aventó contra la estufa.*

Mi amá told me she crawled into a ball against the corner of the wall and the stove. *Le dio la espalda a mi apá,* covering her swollen belly with her arms. So my father just kicked her further into the corner. He was dressed in his best for the night out. *Me imagino verlo muy guapo, con la ropa que mi ama le plancho antes de salir. Una camisa vaquera de manga larga, pantalones de mesclilla y acampanados.*

You remember ever seeing those kinds of pants? Snug bellbottomed trousers, ironed with a perfect line down the front of each leg. *Mi amá se los planchaba con mucho cuidado porque asi le gustaba a mi papa.* And the thick leather belt and shiny leather cowboy boots. *Con las puntas agudas.* Pointy hard leather at the toe of the boot. *Como dice el dicho, «mi mamá vestia al mono pa' que otras lo vailaran.»*

Pues con eso le daba las patadas a mi amá. He kicked her with those shiny boots until he got tired.

Ay solo ellos dos saben cuanto duro. Cuantas patadas le dió.

Mi ama wasn't able to protect her whole belly. So the baby must have felt the blows. *Y el llanto de mi ama.* Her begging for mercy.

«Por favor, Romulo! ¡Por el bebé que viene! Ya no...»

So Challo was born with a map on his back. Thankfully, over time, his bruises also faded.

Ay, mi apá. Porque tenia que ser haci. I was two years away, you know. I hadn't yet met my father.

¿Y mis moretes? Son invicibles. They may never disappear.

La verdad aveces duele. *Sí. Haci es. Y aunque no me guste, estoy aquí gracias a mi padre. Tambien el me hizo.* I am here, in part because of my father. *El tiempo no pasa en vano.* He risked his life for us. To give us a better life.
Pues si. It's really hard to forget. *Y mucho menos perdonar.*
I love my father.

***

This text was the foundation for a teatro performance developed as part of the Undocumented Lives Performance Workshop directed by Maestra Cherríe Moraga in February 2013 and performed at the Nitery Theatre, Stanford University and the Brava Theatre, San Francisco, CA.

leave

mami, we need to leave daddy
yes, baby, we will leave him
too many broken promises
so i left first

vamos

mami, tenemos que dejar a mi apá
si, mija, lo dejaremos
demasiadas promesas sin cumplir
así que primero me fui yo

Chapter 4: New York

humility

before Stanford and Harvard
i was a laborer
pesticide exposed
asthma induced

i cleaned other people's toilets
swept and mopped floors
polished shoes, furniture
cooked, washed, fed

i took care of other people's children
i hoped
i loved

abusive working conditions were the norm
a matter of survival
choices were limited
i couldn't breathe

i was a mother in a family i did not create
my parents were like children
i wasted time breaking up fights
my father was abusive
my mother let him

before Stanford and Harvard
i was hungry for freedom

during Stanford and Harvard
i was a laborer
pesticide exposed
asthma induced

abusive learning conditions were the norm
a matter of survival
choices were limited
i couldn't breathe

but i found an extended family
a critical mass of community
trying to balance educational attainment
with the pursuit of justice

during Stanford and Harvard
i starved for freedom

after Stanford and Harvard
i am a different kind of laborer
pesticide exposed
asthma induced

i still take care of other people's children
i hope
i love

after Stanford and Harvard
i have tasted many freedoms
but liberation is yet to come

humildad

antes de Stanford y Harvard
fui campesina
expuesta a los pesticidas
afectada con asma

limpie baños ajenos
barrí y trapié pisos
pulí zapatos, muebles
cociné, lavé, alimenté

cuidé niños ajenos
esperé
amé

abusivas condiciones de trabajo eran común
tenía que sobrevivir
puras opciones limitadas
no podía respirar

fui mamá en una familia que no diseñé
mis padres eran como niños
perdí el tiempo parando peleas
mi padre era abusivo
mi madre lo dejaba

antes de Stanford y Harvard
sentía hambre por la libertad

durante Stanford y Harvard
fui campesina
expuesta a las pesticidas
afectada con asma

abusivas condiciones de aprendizaje eran común
tenía que sobrevivir
puras opciones limitadas
no podía respirar

pero encontré una familia extensa
una comunidad crítica
intentando balancear logros académicos
con el propósito de la justicia

durante Stanford y Harvard
yo me moría de hambre por la libertad

después de Stanford y Harvard
soy campesina diferente
expuesta a los pesticidas
afectada con asma

sigo cuidando niños ajenos
espero
amo

después de Stanford y Harvard
he probado muchas libertades
pero todavía no llega la liberación

class of '99

Harvard graduation
two girls, chicanas, first-generation
the sisters
Stanford BAs
now completing Masters
we offered to pay for his airfare
so many excuses, started a fight
he didn't attend our graduation
my sister is still angry
i guess he had better things to do

clase del '99

graduación de Harvard
dos muchachas, chicanas, primera generación
las hermanas
licenciaturas de Stanford
ahora completando maestrías
ofrecimos pagar su vuelo
tuvo muchas excusas, comenzó una pelea
él no asisitió a nuestra graduación
mi hermana todavía está sentida
supongo que él tenía mejores cosas que hacer

nyc

a few years ago
i ran away from home
i ran away from pain
sadness
my family
comfort
success
community
my people

i was looking for myself
my joy
a personal challenge
internal knowledge
a new experience

i stumbled upon
a different version of
pain
sadness
my family
comfort
success
community
my people

my spiritual evolution
an emotional and sexual revolution
a butterfly emerged from its cocoon

i found love
my love
for me

ciudad de nueva york

hace unos años
huí de mi casa
huí del dolor
la tristeza
mi familia
la comodidad
el éxito
la comunidad
mi gente

me buscaba a mi misma
mi alegría
un desafío personal
entendimiento interno
una experiencia nueva

me tropecé
con una versión diferente
del dolor
la tristeza
mi familia
la comodidad
el éxito
la comunidad
mi gente

mi evolución espiritual
una revolución emocional y sexual
una mariposa salio de su capullo

encontré el amor
mi propio amor
para mi

easter 2003

impromptu family meeting
started with a fight
my younger siblings argued
who is going to take care of mom and dad?
the girls have always done it
we're tired
the boys hadn't tried
my younger sister shared frustrations, cried, vented
my younger brother shared rage, cried, vented
i tried to be always understanding
big brother was born that day
sister, tell us what you are feeling?
i shrunk, dumbfounded, words stumbled
a waterfall of tears and lament
i don't want to be the momma anymore
i am tired of being the momma
to you
to mom and dad
to everyone but myself
i don't want to be the momma anymore
i want to be the baby now
they all stared
in unison, okay

pascua 2003

una imprevista junta familiar
comenzó con un disgusto
mis hermanos menores alegaban
¿quién va a cuidar de mamá y papá?
las muchachas siempre lo han hecho
estamos cansadas
los muchachos no han hecho esfuerzo
mi hermana menor compartió frustraciones, lloró, se desahogó
mi hermano menor compartió rabia, lloró, se desahogó
yo siempre intente ser comprensiva
hermano mayor nació ese día
¿hermana, dinos lo que sientes?
me encogí, atontada, las palabras tropezaron
una cascada de lagrimas y lamentos
ya no quiero ser la mamá
estoy cansada de ser la mamá
de ustedes
de mamá y papá
de todos menos de mi misma
ya no quiero ser la mamá
ahora quiero ser la baby
todos se me quedaron viendo
juntos, de acuerdo.

the baby

i have an announcement to make
i am the baby now
that means everybody does what i say
and i get my way
friends laugh, know that i am joking
but not really

they support me in this new endeavor
to take care of me
with the same determination and drive
used to take care of everyone else
taking baby steps, stumbling, slow
but i am not afraid
because i am no longer alone

la baby

tengo un anuncio que hacer
ahora yo soy la baby
eso significa que todo el mundo hace lo que digo
y me salgo con la mía
mis amigos se ríen, saben que estoy bromeando
pero en realidad no

me apoyan en este nuevo emprendimiento
para cuidar de mí
con la misma determinación y ganas
con las que cuidaba a los demás
tomando pasos de bebé, tropezando, lentamente
pero no tengo miedo
porque ya no estoy sola

take out the trash

i am no longer a child
defenseless and alone
i can choose
i will not accept violence
my spirit, mind, and body are precious

i decided
my mirror will not reflect hate
i am everything i need

i cannot change the past
so i relish my strength
and let go of innocence lost

i decided
to stop hurting myself
by harboring nightmares

i will not give audience to insanity

my father's curse
my uncle's unsolicited touch
my lovers' inadequacies
any refusal to take care of me
has been wrapped in black plastic
and disposed

saca la basura

ya no soy niña
indefensa y sola
puedo escoger
no voy aceptar la violencia
mi espíritu, mente y cuerpo son preciosos

decidí
mi espejo no reflejará odio
yo soy todo lo que necesito

no puedo cambiar el pasado
así que disfruto mi fuerza
y dejo ir la inocencia perdida

decidí
dejar de hacerme daño
al guardar pesadillas

no dare audencia a la locura

la maldición de mi padre
el tacto insolicitado de mi tío
las faltas de mis amantes
cualquier rehúso a cuidarme
se ha envuelto en plástico negro
y se ha dispuesto

my students

three little girls
sisters
PreK, kindergarten, first grade
first grade has welts lining her back
she tells her teacher she fell down the stairs
the school nurse inspects the bruises
somebody calls children's services
they intend to remove the girls without notifying the parents
mom's boyfriend is suspect
mom's own bruises have not gone unnoticed
children's services is going to take the girls away
the girls are calm
they have seen this before
kindergarden tries to comfort first grade
she sings, no more bruises…
mom arrives before the girls leave
children's services is not prepared
hysteria ensues
why are you taking my daughters?!
i place my hand on her shoulder
please, mom, think of your children
she calms down and says goodbye
she looks like an older sister
kissing each baby as she helps put on their coats
boyfriend calls incessantly
she pleads with him over the phone
don't bring the baby here, or they will take him away too!
hours later
the nurse's office is a waiting room
children's services gives the final go ahead
mom is inconsolable
the police officer escorts her out
the girls say goodbye
they will meet in court the next day
it will be months before i allow myself to cry
over three little girls
i will never see again

mis estudiantes

tres niñas
hermanitas
pre-kinder, kinder, y primer grado
primer grado tiene moretes por la espalda
le dice a la maestra que se cayó por las escaleras
la enfermera de la escuela inspecciona los moretes
alguien llama a servicios sociales
piensan llevarse a las niñas sin notificar a los padres
el novio de mamá es sospechoso
los moretes de mamá no han pasado sin notarse
servicios sociales se van a llevar a las niñas
las niñas están calmadas
han visto esto antes
kinder trata de confortar a primer grado
le canta, no más moretes...
mamá llega antes de que se lleven a las niñas
servicios sociales no están preparados
histeria sobreviene
¿¡por qué se llevan a mis hijas!?
pongo mi mano en su hombro
por favor, mamá, piense en sus niñas
se calma y se despide
parece hermana mayor
besando cada nena al ponerles las chamarras
el novio llama sin cesar
ella le suplica por el teléfono
¡por favor no traigas al bebé, o se lo llevaran a el también!
horas después
la oficina de la enfermera se convierte en sala de espera
servicios sociales da la última orden
mamá esta inconsolable
el policía la acompaña a la salida
las niñas se despiden
se verán en corte al día siguiente
pasarán meses antes de que pueda llorar
por tres hermanitas
que nunca volveré a ver

angels

there are children who suffer
who beg for love and affection from relative strangers
who get used to being left behind and forgotten
who are teased for "smelling funny"
who wear the same soiled clothes multiple days in a row
who walk the streets at all hours
who are brilliant in the face of misery

angeles

hay niños que sufren
que suplican por amor y cariño de desconocidos
que se acostumbran a ser olvidados
que reciben burla porque huelen raro
que llevan la mismo ropa sucia día tras día
que caminan por la calle a todas horas
que aluzan el cielo al encarar la miseria

Chapter 5: *Reflejos*

poem for words

i really like words
colors, music, and feeling can be expressed by words very eloquently
words can inspire a vision of joy so overwhelming
i sometimes think i could fall in love with words
but, of course, that is easier said than done
to fall in love with words would require that i trust in the power of words to express true
emotional investment
i think this is too heavy for words
words can incite deep pleasure and yet create a sense of loss and pain that is beyond words
words can be beautiful, expressing a multitude of qualities that are utterly attractive
words can stimulate my intellectual, emotional, and physical senses
words can create a picture, feeling, a smell i can almost touch
i can taste words salty sweet aroma on the tip of my tongue
but i have to keep words at arms length
to find release at the tips of my fingers
only on the surface
because what if i let words get the best of me
and find there isn't enough in words to show me love?
i do not want to be at a loss for words
heart-broken and tongue-tied
by words inability to fulfill my needs
for the perfect words to manifest my dreams
i sometimes think i could fall in love with words
because i know there is a great deal of potential in words
i have seen words evolve
but until i can trust that words will be strong enough to show true
affection, tenderness, and passion

for me
for now
i will only say
i really like words

sangria

a perfect glass of sangria
in a roomful of watered down rum
everyone was thirsty
scampering for instant gratification
unwilling to savor quality

the sangria had it all
succulent fruit
a flawless blend of juice
and sweet red wine
a california special label

it was too much for the masses
content with mediocrity
and consumption of the
inadequate, diluted familiar

the sangria was different
a single glass
able to elicit clarity of thought and
communal lucidity for those who were willing
to work for the prize

some had hope of discerning taste
but were easily overwhelmed by sheer quantity
of a cheap means to a drunken stupor
that lets them believe they are satisfied

outnumbered by those desiring an easy high
the sangria refused to linger
and walked into the crisp night air
heals clicking on the pavement
as she strutted off in joy
to a better party

sangría

una perfecta copa de sangría
en un salón lleno de ron desabrido
todos tenían sed
buscaban gratificación instantánea
sin querer saborear calidad

la sangría lo tenia todo
fruta suculenta
una combinación sin falla de jugo
y dulce vino rojo
etiqueta especial de california

era demasiado para la muchedumbre
contentos con lo mediocre
y consumo de lo
inadecuado, diluido familiar

la sangría era diferente
solamente una copa
pero capaz de provenir claridad de pensamiento
y lucidez comunal para los que se atrevieran
a trabajar por el premio

los que tuvieron esperanza de derivar sabor
se asombraron con la excesiva cantidad
escogieron la manera fácil de embriagarse
que les permite creer que están satisfechos

con tantos persiguiendo un embriago fácil
la sangría decidió no quedarse
salió hacia el aire limpio de la noche
tacones palpitando por el pavimento
mientras caminaba con gusto
hacia una fiesta más divertida

wake up

i had a nightmare
my baby brother is being slaughtered
a perfect slit from throat to core
two men stand by and watch
as he struggles to hold onto his insides
i know these men
i have been with them
they stare, frozen as my brother bleeds

they claim he was willing
deny responsibility
as they wash their hands with his blood

disgusted by their compliance
i refuse to hear excuses

i leave them to look for help
shocked by the violence of my words

i wake up

older brother interprets my dream
baby brother represents you
your spirit is trying to tell you
these men hurt you
stop acting like it is okay
accept your rage
let them go

he is right
i love my baby brother
i helped raise him
cared for him when nobody else could

i had to ask myself why
my reaction would have been less visceral
if i had been the victim in my dream

despierta

tuve una pesadilla
mi hermanito menor está siendo sacrificado
una cortada liza de garganta hasta el núcleo
hay dos hombres de pie mirando
mientras lucha por sostener sus entrañas
yo conozco a estos hombres
he estado con ellos
ellos lo miran fijamente, como estatuas, mientras mi hermano sangra

dicen que dio permiso
renuncian toda responsabilidad
mientras se lavan las manos con su sangre

siento asco por su conformidad
me niego a oír excusas

los dejo para buscar ayuda
sorprendida por la violencia de mis palabras

me despierto

hermano mayor interpreta mi sueño
hermano menor te representa a ti
tu espíritu intenta decirte
esos hombres te hicieron daño
deja de actuar como si no importa
acepta tu coraje
déjalos ir

tiene razón
yo adoro a mi hermanito
ayudé a crearlo
lo cuide cuando nadie más pudo

tuve que preguntarme por qué
mi reacción habría sido menos visceral
si yo hubiera sido la víctima en mi sueño

reflection

i can talk about it now
for a long time
i was a bad friend
i stood by and watched
my heart get broken

surrounded by haters
i picked me last

i cried for me
i wanted to give up
i knew i could be more
so i stopped waiting

let go of silence
rage and disappointment
i demanded respect

i remember the shock
my soul revealed
being honest with yourself is difficult
the facade finally crumbled
i decided to change

i am smarter and stronger
looking out for me every day
everything i ever wanted
beautiful, powerful, compassionate

i bloom in my sunshine

my reflection

i look in the mirror
and i know love

reflejo

ahora lo puedo admitir
por mucho tiempo
fui mala amiga
no me defendía
cuando me rompían el corazón

rodeada de odiosos
nunca me escogí

yo lloraba por mi misma
me quise dar por vencida
sabía que podía ser más
así que dejé de esperar

dejé ir el silencio
rabia y decepción
exigí respeto

recuerdo el choque
que mi alma reveló
ser honesta con si misma es difícil
la farsa finalmente se cayó
decidí cambiar

soy más inteligente y más fuerte
me cuido todos los días
soy todo lo que siempre quise
hermosa, poderosa, compasiva

floreo en mi luz

mi reflejo

me miro en el espejo
y conozco el amor

truth

i have to be honest
i see you watching me
an open book
for my reading pleasure

i have to be honest
i have been chasing you
looking for your potential
so much promise
yet unfulfilled

i see you watching me
i am the truth you desire
but i am too far away
from your comfort zone

we both agree
it could be wonderful
i love forward movement
and so do you
but the pace of our stride differs
along this uncertain road

can we handle it?
i think I can
you can't, or won't

i have to be honest
life is too short
and i refuse to waste time

i see you watching me
will you see the truth
as i walk away
or after i'm gone?

la verdad

tengo que ser honesta
te veo mirándome
un libro abierto
para leer con placer

tengo que ser honesta
te he estado persiguiendo
buscando tu potencial
tanta promesa
todavía sin cumplir

te veo mirándome
soy la verdad que deseas
pero estoy muy lejos
de tu zona confortable

estamos de acuerdo
que podría ser maravilloso
yo adoro el progreso
y tu también
pero el compás de nuestro handar es distinto
por este camino incierto

¿podemos lograrlo?
yo creo que puedo
tu no puedes, o no quieres

tengo que ser honesta
la vida es demasiado corta
y no quiero perder tiempo

te veo mirándome
te darás cuenta de la verdad
¿cuando me empiece alejar
o cuando ya no esté?

insufficient

i was catatonic for weeks
after i decided to let you go

i knew all along
you were not enough
i told you
too many secrets

you sent me a bouquet of silence
petals every shade of gray
fulfilled my lowest expectations

you made breaking my heart look easy
turned your back
dropped lead on my chest
until everything inside collapsed

you were not an easy lesson

time, energy, and love spent
on self-centered, immature selfishness

no thanks

i want somebody extraordinary
somebody stronger and ready to live
somebody more like me

insuficiente

estuve atónica por varias semanas
después que decidí dejarte ir

lo supe siempre
no eras suficiente
te dije
demasiados secretos

me mandaste un ramo de silencio
pétalos en cada tono de gris
cumpliste mis más bajas expectativas

se te hizo fácil romper mi corazón
me diste la espalda
dejaste caer plomo sobre mi pecho
hasta que mi interior se derrumbó

no fuiste lección fácil

tiempo, energía y amor gastado
en un egoísta e inmaduro llorón

no gracias

yo quiero alguien extraordinario
más fuerte y preparado para vivir
alguien que sea más como yo

i am not the one

you often forget
i never hurt you
you often forget
i am not the one

who left you empty
took you for granted
broke your heart

you squander my love
on superficial pleasures
misdirected anger
and blind fear

you often forget
i never hurt you
you often forget
i was the one

who cherished you
shared my sunshine
gave you strength

one day you'll be able
to look in the mirror
and let go of hate

you will remember
i never hurt you
when it's too late

i deleted you

i dreamt you
again
and woke
this morning
overwhelmed
with desire
to
make you
disappear

i picked up my phone
my heart
filled with peace
and i deleted you

i used to crave
your scent
your skin
your touch

today
i am repulsed
by the sound
of your name

i yearn
to be free
of your pain
grief
and moody selfishness
to delight
in the light
and joy
that blossoms
in your absence

i want
to delete

your memory
to remove
your mark
from my cells
to erase
our
story

i can no longer
hold you
help you
give you
love

i refuse
to carry
your shadow

i am grateful
for the ebb
of time
a tide
that washes you away
every second
a gift
i am renewed
my life
moves forward

you
will
never
catch
up

i deleted you today

viejo arrastrado

¡pinche viejo arrastrado!
i'm finally free
porque yo quiero
i choose to be

in love with life
in love with me

tu me dejaste
gracias a Dios
me hiciste un favor
i love me more

sin tu desastre
i'm drama free
ya me cansaste
i'm done with crazy

te quise mucho
but now i'm free
porque yo quiero
i choose to be

in love with life
in love with me

el mosquito muerto

eres un mosquito muerto
y asi vaz a quedar

Chapter 6: *Besitos*

circle of fire

yo soy chicana
de califaztlan
equal parts *las animas, nochiztlan, zacatecas*
y el orranteño, saucillo, chihuahua
pero born and raised in the grape fields of the central valley
una mujer del rancho
with an urban sensibility

i survived the farm
and rode the crimson tide
over ivy walls
antes de morder la gran manzana
where i, also grew up
before coming to *tejas*
de un rancho a otro

but it's hotter than hell here
the original ring of fire
como mi favorito chile de árbol
que me hace hasta llorar
but i keep coming back for more
because somehow
without the burn
my food just doesn't taste right

i am a california girl
una chicana de califaztlan
with a new appreciation for tight jeans and work boots

as much as for the baggy pants and fly kicks
of my west coast, east coast past
and likely future
pero aquí estoy ahora
en el corazón de tejas
bailando con el diablo
y sus compadres

¡me estoy quemando!
pero me gusta
porque aunque no soy tejana
también soy chingona
and i can handle the heat

revolution

you were birthed by a woman
just like my mother
but showered in privilege
i recognize

illegitimate power
sedates your conscience
erases our history
silences your heart

your ignorance has purpose
to render invisible
mutilated flesh
hungry mouths
battered souls

your hatespeak and greed
breeds a discourse of chaos
pillages dignity
plunders bodies
poisons the earth

so many reasons
to call you my enemy
yet, i refuse

this is my revolution
the will to educate
to hold your hand
to see your humanity
is linked to my own

you were birthed by a woman
just like my mother
to dismantle your privilege
i must recognize

i speak the truth of your violence
in search of redemption
i pray for the courage
to still wish you love

revolución

naciste de un a mujer
igual que mi madre
pero bañado en privilegio
lo reconozco

el poder ilegitimo
sedó tu conciencia
borra nuestra historia
silencia tu corazón

tu ignorancia tiene propósito
de hacer invisible
piel mutilada
bocas hambrientas
almas azotadas

tus palabras de odio y egoísmo
crean discurso de caos
pillaja la dignidad
devasta cuerpos
envenena la tierra

tantas razones
para llamarte mí enemigo
pero me rehúso

esta es mi revolución
el deseo de educar
de tomar tu mano
de ver que tu humanidad
también es la mía

naciste de una mujer
igual que mi madre
para desbaratar tu privilegio
tengo que reconocer

hablo la verdad de tu violencia
en busca de la redención
y rezo por el valor
de aun desearte amor

alternative love

this adventure is a dream
where we explore
alternative love
passion, friendship, trust
we agree
to redefine
possibilities
safety, comfort, freedom

like no one before
i let you
enter my core
and feed my breath
with fluid motion

we come
from different eras
of time and space
you are the past
i am the future
we meet in the present
here, now

you seek me out
i make myself available
repeatedly, easily
effortless words erupt
for you

a unique experience
for both

i cherish you
and our freedom
to choose
the beginning
and end

of this alternative
love

amor alternativo

esta aventura es un sueño
donde exploramos
amor alternativo
pasión, amistad, confianza
estamos de acuerdo
al redefinir
posibilidades
protección, consuelo, libertad

como a nadie antes
te permito
penetrar mi interior
y alimentar mis suspiros
con movimiento fluido

venimos
de diferentes eras
de tiempo y espacio
tu eres el pasado
yo soy el futuro
nos conocemos en el presente
aquí, ahora

tu me buscas
yo me dejo encontrar
repetidamente, fácil
palabras sin esfuerzo brotan
para ti

un experiencia única
para ambos

te quiero a ti
y a nuestra libertad
de escoger
el principio
y el fin

de este amor
alternativo

¿qué significa amarte?

me dejo llevar por la corriente
que me hace latir a tu compás
aterrada, feliz y desorientada
quiero ser tuya, de nadie más

me llevas a la sima del precipicio
una barranca sin fondo
donde me dejo caer una y otra vez

te entrego todo, mi piel, mi alma
mi sanidad, sin condición
eres siempre mi derrota
y también mi salvación

soporto el dolor de tu ausencia
esta locura no tiene fin
me desconozco en tu presencia
lo aguanto todo por tenerte aquí

estoy dispuesta a morir despacio
mi ser se aleja de mi interior
rompo el cordón de mis entrañas
y abandono lo conocido
por entrar en tu dimensión

me siento tonta y intoxicada
mi lucidez desapareció
no quiero dejar este embriago
tu diferencia es mi seducción

¿qué significa amarte?

olvidar las pesadillas
enfrentar a mis fantasmas
desalojar mi egoísmo
hacerte campo en mi corazón

por mis ojos

te tengo cerca
mi amor amigo
and i am not afraid
ya una vez
me rompiste
el alma
sin querer

i let you take my breath
my lungs crumpled
i collapsed
broken in sorrow
but i survived
and birthed again

i can love you still
i can choose to hold your hand
while you learn to love yourself

¿por qué quiero?
porque puedo
y no tengo miedo
perderte

i am free
i will not
shatter
for you
again

si te acercas
es porque quieres
you must not be afraid
courage is contagious
como mi amor, amigo
con respeto y compasión

si te pudieras ver por mis ojos
conocerías la paz
porque mi amor, amigo
es liberación

tu alma me encuentra

tu alma me encuentra
a través de la tierra
arena y agua salada
mil sueños sin fin

tu suspiro es el mio
alimentas mi aliento
entrelazado en mi carne
más alla del saber

te escucho en el viento
susurro entre las arboledas
el canto en sus hojas
mi nombre en tu voz

despierta el recuerdo
amanecer en tus brazos
el calor de mi sangre
en el rubor de tu piel

nuestro amor es salvaje
deseo y tormenta
nos desgarra y nos mata
y nos hace nacer

atraviesas montes y llanos
para llegar a mi puerto
navegamos distancia
sin temor al dolor

sin vergüenza ninguna
me haces siempre tu espejo
un complicado reflejo
de tu incansable pasión

tu navegaste mi mapa
tierra y mar de mi cuerpo

mi ser y mi sentimiento
esta marcado en tu amor

a kiss

delicious
who knew?
menthol smooth
soft, firm, sweet
pressure
a gentle bite
give
take
give
upper lip
lower flesh
blood rushing
a flush in every cell
feels like seconds ago
blushing in silence
moments relished
but insufficient
and your taste lingers no more

un beso

delicioso
¿quién sabía?
lizo mentol
suave, firme, dulce
presión
una mordidita
dando
recibiendo
dando
labio superior
piel interior
sangre corriendo
un rubor en cada célula
parece que fuera ahora
sonrogiendo en silencio
momentos disfrutados
pero insuficientes
y tu sabor desapareció

Chapter 7: Amig@s

El Higo

One of my favorite childhood games was climbing and playing in an old fig tree that stood behind *la casita blanca*. I can see its beautiful mottled branches from the one window of *el cuartito* overlooking the western horizon from *la casita. Sus ramas eran fuertes y seguras.* I could spend hours in its sprawling shade, arms wrapped around the thick solid trunk and my legs hanging off the gnarled branches of smooth grey wood twisting this way and that towards the sky. The fig's enormous branches hold the weight of three children: Challo, Linda, and me. My siblings and I run to the tree when we have the opportunity to escape from our daily chores and labor. We climb into *el higo* and let our imaginations soar. We take turns transforming *el higo* into the vehicle of our dreams.

"Let's pretend we are on a train, and we can travel anywhere in the world."

"Choo Choo!"

"No, if we want to travel anywhere in the world, it is better if we are in an airplane!" I stretch out my arms to the sky making wings out of them in an effort to show what our plane travel looks like.

Challo has the best idea. «*No, mejor ay que jugar a que es un* spaceship *y haci podemos viajar hasta la luna u otros planetas!*»

«*Está bueno. ¿Listos?* » "Countdown. 10! 9! 8! 7!...."

We yell over each other trying to get to the next number first.

"…6! 5! 4! 3! 2! 1!... Blastoff!!"

Woooooo….we move our arms as if flying along con *el higo*—our spaceship to the moon.

«¿Cómo es la gente en la luna? ¿En otros planetas?»

"We are all the same. *No hay gente pobre. ¡No hay files!*"

We dream in daylight about the wonderful places we can visit, and we talk about what it will be like when we are older, and we leave the confines of our small town.

"We will be able to go to the movies any time we want."

«Sí, y luego vamos a poder ir a comer a restaurantes de verdad, y a comprar ropa nueva.»

«Cuando vallamos a la escuela y ganemos más dinero les vamos a ayudar a mamá y papá a comprar una casa.»

"We no longer have to work in the fields!"

Our adventures are multiplied every time we climb that tree. We each have a place to sit in its branches, smooth strong arms holding us off the earth. The tree provides shade and enclosure, and a sense of safety as we travel the Universe of our childhood fantasies. *El higo es nuestra nave, nuestro hogar, durante los ratos que pasamos en sus ramas.* We find shade in its dark green broad leaves, and when the fruit ripens, we pluck each fig off the branch closest to our reach, savoring the rich jammy sweetness of deep violet flesh mixed with tiny seeds. We help *mami* pick the fruit, and she makes jam for toast with peanut butter or fresh flour tortillas right off the *comal*. I love fresh ripe figs, and the jam *mami* makes is a special treat. In my grownup years I will seek but miserably fail to relive that texture and freshness of unique flavor with fig newtons from the grocery store. *Ese sabor, esas aventuras son solo un recuerdo.* A lasting yet fleeting memory of a fruit that fed our dreams of escape from the reality of our childhood of poverty and violence.

I miss *el higo*, and I wish I could return to those welcoming branches. However, when *la casita* was condemned, everything was destroyed. The tree, like the house, was uprooted and demolished into shreds of splintered wood and clumps of earth. *El higo* was home to our dreams of freedom and adventure. We rode its branches away from Reedley and far away into the horizon many years after it was pulled from the earth.

Rascuache Navidad

For many years my father brings home our Christmas tree from the peach and plum orchards where he prunes during the winter. He cannot afford to buy us a real Christmas tree, so he brings home a large branch that he has shaped with his pruning shears. The tree is inverted in many ways. It has no leaves, no green pine needles. The branches face upwards like arms reaching for the sky. I am embarrassed and excited at the same time. Embarrassed that our tree is "poor" and not like the Christmas trees we have at school. But I am also excited about decorating our own tree, especially because *mami* works so hard with my siblings and me. She is so excited, and I live to see her happy, so I want to make it look as pretty as possible. *Mami* feeds our creativity and helps us make use of what we have at home and the few decorations we make at school, during arts and crafts. *Mami's* ability to make something out of nothing rubs off on all of us. We recycle construction paper and make chains out of red and green links of paper. She wraps the brown dead branches in aluminum foil and we make homemade ornaments out of leftover sheets of paper from our homework assignments. She shows us how to cut up egg cartons and also wrap them in aluminum foil. We hang these upside down to look like bells swinging on the branches. *Mami* buys one set of red *esferas* at the local discount store. She convinces my father to buy us one string of silver tinsel and a string of lights. We manage to use these for many years. Everything else is homemade.

My *nina* and her kids come over to see our tree. They tell us how original it is, and this makes my mother so happy that I am filled with pride and a sense of accomplishment. It is a time of year when our poverty becomes more prevalent, and we are made aware of how much we do not have. But it is also a time when we have fun with each other and try to do the best with what we do have. We sleep together on the living room floor of the mobile home, and we have slumber parties between the five of us, *mami*, Challo, Linda, Rómulo, and me. Our mobile home does not have central heating, so we huddle together around our one space heater and drink *té de canela or chocolate caliente*. We watch reruns of "Rudolf the Red Nosed Reindeer" and "*Marcelino Pan y Vino*" on the twelve-inch black and white television set. My father is usually with us on Christmas morning, when we pass around the gifts we get from "*el niño Dios*". Our presents are not many, but they are things we each need. A pair of socks. A pair of pants. A new shirt or sweater. So we can go back to school in January with something "new". My *nina* also always thinks of us. Even though she is my godmother, she always brings a gift for each of my siblings as well.

One year my father is in Mexico during the holidays. He is working on getting his U.S. residency and ends up staying away for six months. We are without a father again, and it is a difficult time for us. None of us kids are old enough to drive and *mami* never learned. We are not able to work while he is gone, and *mami* has to ask one of his uncles to lend us money. Economically, it was one of the worst winters for us, but we still managed to find many moments of joy. Our father is away. We are free from his unpredictable moments of rage and violence, and we enjoy each other tremendously. That year *mami* is not able to get us any gifts, but we still put up our rascuache tree. And we sleep together on the living room floor to wait for "*el niño Dios*".

We wake up Christmas morning, and the space under the tree is still empty. Challo gets dressed slowly and walks outside to feed the animals. He finds a large cardboard box on the staircase leading to the front door of our mobile home. He brings it inside and sets it on the living room floor. We stand around and watch as *mami* opens the box. It is full of wrapped gifts! We pass them around, laughing and crying in amazement. I have never seen so many toys before. We never find out who put that box outside our door, and I know I will remember that Christmas morning for the rest of my life.

Turtle Memory

She came from Cali to Texas with her beautiful rich brown shell covered in *turquesa* and beaded with images of the places she has traveled, and the places she has yet to reach. There is a story written in those images on her shell, the home she takes with her everywhere she goes. She has always been a turtle but when she left Cali she was also layered in rabbit fur. It was colder there, and she needed the extra layers. But in Texas, it's really hot, so the fur had to come off along with the layers that helped her survive a different time and place.

Texas is usually pretty flat but this turtle cowgirl from Cali went to the one place in the big ol' state where you have to climb. They call it hill country. She finds this funny because it looks more like ant hills. Anyway, there is one hill in this crazy land that is really kind of big. It is unnatural, I tell you. This hill is very popular and many people try to climb it. The hill is beautiful in its own way, but it is covered in obstacles, you know, "bumps in the road," as they say. Because when you get to the top of the hill you get a paper that says you are gifted and talented and deserving of other privileges.

Well, the cowgirl turtle from Cali knows she is already gifted and talented and deserving of all the beautiful riches of the world. Yet, she wants to climb that hill anyway simply because not that many turtles like her have done it before and there are these crazy bald headed vultures that believe beautiful brown turtles like her should not even get the chance. So she decided many moons ago that those vultures can go to hell because she is going to get up that darn hill no matter what. So she climbs and climbs and climbs, and she takes her sweet time because she is a turtle after all and nobody is going to make her mess up her beautiful brown shell. Maybe if she ran too fast she might trip and fall and lose those beautiful beads and *turquesa*. So she takes her time because she knows how important these jewels are to keep her shell healthy and strong. This shell is her home, and it keeps her spirit safe, so she must not let it be destroyed.

The beautiful brown turtle climbs and climbs and climbs, and all the time she can see the top of the hill and sometimes she gets really tired and those scary vultures are just hovering around her, and their shadows block out the sun. This beautiful brown cowgirl turtle loves the sun, and she wants to stop and relax and let the sun warm her shell. But those darn vultures will just swoop down and eat her up if she stops too long. So even though she gets really tired and sometimes even sad because she misses the beautiful water from where she came, she knows she has to keep going.

After many moons have passed she realizes she is almost there, and she can see there are others like her at the top of the hill. Beautiful brown turtles, with different kinds of shells, because they have different kinds of strength and need different kinds of homes. And she sees that these other turtles have made a path that she can follow. So she keeps climbing and climbing and climbing. Slow and steady. And even when she just wants to give up, and those vultures are just circling in, she feels a soft breeze that lifts her spirit and gives her wings.

She looks around and sees the spirits of her turtle brothers and sisters. Some of them are those that are already on the top of the hill. Yet, they let their spirits join her so that she can come up and play with them. One little turtle is carrying a guitar and he looks tired and his spirit takes the form of a snake. She sees he is shedding his skin and even though this is painful to witness, something about him gives her strength. Maybe she sees some hope in that little turtle, and she knows what it feels like to struggle and overcome, to shed your skin over and over until you find the real you. Even though she has already passed that part of the hill herself, she knows it is important to be reminded of the bumps she left behind. Then there is this super cute light brown turtle with honey eyes. His spirit takes the form of a horse, and he is wearing cowboy boots and a hat. She sees that he is strong and fearless and generous with his strength. He knows the path well and he shows her where to go. She takes the strength he offers, and she pushes forward. Then there is also another beautiful brown turtle from Cali who takes the form of a tiger. Her spirit is also strong and fearless. She roars at the vultures when they get too close and they fly away because she can be scary when in full rage. But her voice is also soft and encour-aging, and she whispers into her friend's ear and reminds her of her beauty and strength and the many gifts and talents she has brought with her from the water and mountains of Cali. So the beautiful brown cowgirl turtle from Cali remembers, like a song recorded into the very fibers of her shell, that she is not alone. Her friends' and families' spirits are always with her and this gives her warmth and energy and love, and she keeps climbing and climbing up that hill.

On the other side of the hill is a gorgeous powerful buck, also climbing and pushing, and reaching for his own joy at the top of the hill. That is where they will meet and everyone will celebrate the beautiful brown cowgirl turtle from Cali and all will recharge from her beauty and strength and the example she has set because they realize that there are always hills in each of their voyages and at different times they each need the help and guidance of the others. In the moment of gathering and celebration every turtle knows that as long as spirits can touch each other and share love, they will always keep climbing, and at their own pace, they will each reach the top.

Dreams

I was sitting in a restaurant with two of my closest girlfriends when I was overwhelmed with the many blessings in my life. They were planning my birthday celebration and asked me to excuse myself to the ladies room so they could talk about the plans. I happily acquiesced, thrilled that making my birthday special was so important to them. We had a wonderful meal together, enjoying each other's company, and sharing the latest stories of our personal voyages in life and love. The conversation was riddled with laughter.

The topic of my birthday got me thinking about my childhood. I was reminded of conversations with my brother when we were young children dreaming of what our lives would be when we grew up. We talked about what we believed to be critical far-away ages. Where would we be when we turned 18, 25, 30? We were farmworker children, laboring in the California grape fields alongside our parents. Our parents ventured to this country from *México* in their youth, seeking a means to the American Dream and a better life for themselves and their family. We worked what felt like endless hours to help our family survive financially. We went to school and sought to excel because we believed it would be the only way out of poverty and constant struggle. There were many moments of sadness and pain, and we had ample reasons to want to dream about what we hoped would be a better time in our lives.

Our dreams were manifested in the form of shared stories, and we played games that reflected those things we most desired. My siblings and I had resourceful imaginations and actively pursued creative outlets as a means to escape our often-bleak reality. We perfected a "restaurant" game with crayons and leftover homework paper. We colored and cut out drawings of the foods we most fantasized being able to buy but knew we couldn't afford. The game consisted of acting like we were in fancy restaurants, ordering and indulging in everything our little hearts and bellies desired. I can still see the sadness in my mother's face when she discovered us in the midst of this wonderful game. It would be many years before I could fully grasp the extent of her anguish over the things she knew neither she nor my father could provide.

My brother and I dreamt aloud about what it would be like to get away from all of the things and places that burdened our hearts. We dreamed of being free. Free from having to work under the sun for meager earnings. Free from my father's critical and irrational guard over our every move. We would get an education and be able to find jobs that made us happy. We would make friends with whomever we wanted and go wherever we wanted, whenever we wanted. We would also be able to take care of ourselves, and eventually our parents.

I am thankful for my education. The experience of attending Stanford and Harvard has enriched my life in more ways than I could have imagined. The education I received outside of the classroom was just as valuable as the academic schooling that resulted in my degrees. One of the two greatest gifts my schooling has provided is the opportunity to learn how to communicate effectively in written form. The other is the ability to think critically about the world I live in, and to challenge myself to put thought into action in a way that is honest, responsible, and considerate of how my choices affect the lives of others. Outside of the classroom, I was bestowed with the gift of friendship, community, identity, and self-respect.

I am thankful for my friends. My education and subsequent career opportunities have provided me with the space to meet and build relationships with people who have filled my life with meaning and love in a way that would not have been possible otherwise. I have met people who inspire me to live in love and laughter. I have friends who hold my hand and my heart every day. People who stand with me in times of sorrow and dance with me in times of joy. I have friends who remind me of the need to celebrate the day of my birth.

I am thankful for my family. My mother, father, brothers, and sister love me. I love them. We tell each other all the time. Not everybody has this. We don't agree about a lot of things. But we get over it when we don't. We look out for each other. We miss each other. We drive each other crazy yet we try not to drive each other away. We sometimes hurt each other, but we also try to make it better. Not everybody has this. I used to believe I had to take care of everybody and that was an impossible way to live. I ran away from my family for a few years. I needed to allow myself to learn how to take care of myself—to love myself as much, and more, than I love my family. They let me go, and they have supported me on this journey. We make each other proud, and we let each other know it.

I have been away from my family in cities that feel like they are on the other side of the world. I left the comfort and security of my friends and family for the opportunity to work with children and youth from life experiences vastly different, and yet all too familiar, to my own. I am an educator. This is a labor of love. There is nothing easy about this. At the same time I am endlessly inspired and filled with hope by my student's resilience and their ability to learn, love, and excel in the face of seemingly insurmountable obstacles.

My life has been a journey of great challenge, and I continue to struggle to heal old wounds on a daily basis. Yet, I have also lived countless experiences of joy that help me face every day with love for others as much as for myself. I have come to learn and deeply believe that Love is my greatest motivator, my reason for getting up every morning with hope and gratitude for a new breath and a new day. So many of my dreams have come true. My chosen career in education, my work with students, my writing and the expression of my stories is much more than labor outside of the fields. It is an offering of Love. I strive to experience and share love every day. Every day. The rush is unbelievable.

luna

my heart was bruised and battered
tissue scarred with broken glass
and shards of memory
cloaked in shadows and nightmares

"i will never love again,"
i thought
letting every vestige
of hope and light
dissolve
into the walls of my armor

lost in a forest of darkness
i floundered and strained
in deepest pools of blue and grey
until i looked into my soul
and asked for help
from all that is
all that was
all that ever will be

in that moment
as if waiting to be called
the moonlight entered
and rose before my eyes
her light soft and warm
against the cold night sky

she picked me
that silly moon
jumped into my lap
and pranced her way
into my soul

finally.
i became undone
by infinite flurries

of warm sandpaper kisses
and joy
exploding in boundless energy
from a tiny body
of smooth velvet
in black and white

the shell around my heart
cracked and splintered
melted into gooey mushiness

the moonlight broke through
with her brilliance
of beauty without words

she brought me back to life
and into love

dance

submerged in whirlpools of melody
laughter drumming in your belly
hips swaying
head thrown back
tears streaming
as notes erupt from your pores

the joy of spiritual catharsis
via physical manifestation
when flesh sways in rhythm
with words of passion, revolution, heartbreak, and love

baila

sumergida en remolinos de melodía
risotadas retumban en tu vientre
caderas meneando
cabeza hacia atrás
lagrimas corriendo
mientras las notas brotan por tus poros

la alegría de catarsis espiritual
vía manifestación física
cuando los muslos se menean al compás
de palabras de pasión, revolución, decilución y amor

friends

you want to be my friend?
cool

my friends
laugh with me
live with me
stand by me
sing to me
dance with me
share with me
talk with me
feel with me

my friends remind me
i'm fabulous
because they are fabulous
smart
compassionate
funny
conscious
strong
confident
original masterpieces

my friends are my family
they understand me
hold me
love me

are you ready?

amigos

¿tu quieres ser mi amigo?
bueno

mis amigos
ríen conmigo
viven conmigo
se paran a mi lado
me cantan
bailan conmigo
comparten conmigo
hablan conmigo
sienten conmigo

mis amigos me recuerdan
que soy fabulosa
porque ellos son fabulosos
inteligentes
compasivos
chistosos
consientes
fuertes
seguros
obras originales

mis amigos son mi familia
ellos me comprenden
me abrazan
me aman

¿estás preparado?

Acknowledgments

First and foremost, I wish to acknowledge the amazing talents and gifts of David Eli Patiño Mejia for helping me manage this book project and of Cesar Armando Torres for developing the cover and layout design. I am so thrilled and proud to work with each of you!

I am eternally grateful for the love and support of mentors who first encouraged me to write the poems and stories included in this collection: Renato I. Rosaldo, Mary Louise Pratt, James M. Montoya, and José E. Limón. I have immense love and respect for each of you, and I thank you for telling me I was a writer and poet before I was able to believe it myself. I am also honored for the opportunity to work with and be inspired by Maestra Cherríe Moraga at Stanford University. Muchísimas gracias Maestra, por compartir su talento, consejos, y espíritu conmigo.

My deepest appreciation and love to my chosen and blood families for your love and support throughout this journey. *Les agradezco de todo corazón. A mi mama y mi papa, Guadalupe Reyes Prieto y Romulo Prieto, les doy gracias por darme vida y por enseñarme el valor del trabajo y el esfuerzo necesario para salir adelante.* A special thank you to Maria Elena Cruz, José Rosario "Challo" Prieto, and Romulo Prieto Jr. for serving as first Readers of the manuscript, to Linda Prieto for your extensive contributions as Copy Editor, and to Renato I. Rosaldo for additional editorial review. Your time, energy, and commitment are a cherished gift, and I thank you also for holding space with me, and for me, during the many challenging moments of reliving memories necessary for the telling of these lived experiences.

Muchísimas gracias to my beautiful comunidad and familia at El Centro Chicano y Latino and Casa Naranja at Stanford University. Working with my professional colleagues and friends, especially Frances Morales and Margaret Sena, in addition to amazing graduate scholars and undergraduate student staff at El Centro and Naranja is a joy I look forward to every day. It is an honor to share my professional journey and daily adventures with each of you. Thank you for inspiring me to work and live in love every day!

Finally, this book project has been greatly blessed by the support and contributions of the following friends and family. *Mil gracias* to each of you for believing in my project and for helping me bring this book to life. I love you very much!

Agustín Rodríguez, Albert Chevez, Aldric Ulep, Alejandra Reynoso, América Reyes, Anne Magnussen, Anthony De Jesus, Araceli Michelle Velázquez, Baldemar Torres,

Brenda Muñoz, Brenda Sendejo, Catherine Meza, Christen Daniel, Clyde Jones, Cristina Salinas, Cynthia Sanchez, Cynthia Cardona & Francisco Javier Valdiosera, Dana Hersh, Diana González, Erica Walker, Ernie Palomino, Frances Morales, Francisco Duenas, George López, Greg Graves, Guadalupe Reyes Prieto, Gun Ho Lee, Hal & Toni Smith, Ignacio & Consuelo Navarro, Jackie Schmidt-Posner, Jackie Cuevas, Jamahn Lee, James Estrella, James M. Montoya, Jeffrey Garcia, Jesus Torres, Jesus Salas, John & Vickie Ramos Harris, Jorge Flores, Jose R. Prieto, Juan Carlos Aguayo, Justin Lin, Karen Acevedo, Karissa Paddie, Kay Luo, Kevin Little, Kristi Losson, Linda & Steve Jackson, Linda Prieto, Lisa Park, Manuel Rosaldo, Maria E. Cruz, Mary Louise Pratt, Matthew Chen, Maureen Phalen, Maya Kratzer, Michael Villa, Najla Gómez, Nikki Williams, Nisrin Omer, Norma González, Ofelia San, Oscar Escobedo, Perla & Roberto Bonilla, Perla Rodríguez, Rebeca Burciaga & David Tremblay, Rebecca Jamil, Rick Yuen, Robert Crews and Margaret Sena, Robert Lucero, Sam Rosaldo, Sandra Rodríguez, Stacy Villalobos, Sunil Saha, Veronica Flores, Victor Villareal, Yifan Mai, Yoseph Semma, Yvette Zepeda.

About the Author

Elvira Prieto was born and raised in California's Central San Joaquin Valley working alongside her parents and siblings in the grape fields and fruit packing sheds of Reedley and surrounding communities in Fresno County. She is the first woman in her family to attend college, receiving her B.A. in Psychology from Stanford University and an Ed.M. in Administration, Planning, and Social Policy from the Harvard Graduate School of Education.

Elvira has worked in higher education, student affairs, academic advising, policy analysis and implementation, and community-based education for over twenty years. She is currently the Assistant Dean for Student Affairs and Associate Director of El Centro Chicano y Latino and Resident Fellow at Casa Naranja at Stanford University. Elvira's writing focuses on the retelling of life *recuerdos* (memories) and *testimonio* with the intention of creating spaces of light, love, and healing for individuals and community.

Made in the USA
San Bernardino, CA
27 January 2018